Environmental Factors in the Design of Building Fenestration

ARCHITECTURAL SCIENCE SERIES

Editor

HENRY J. COWAN

Professor of Architectural Science
University of Sydney

Previously published

Environmental Factors in the Design of Building Fenestration

by

B. P. LIM

Dip.T.C.P., B.Arch., Ph.D., F.R.A.I.A., M.R.I.B.A., M.S.I.A., M.S.I.P.

K. R. RAO

B.Sc., M.Sc., Ph.D., F.Inst.P., M.I.S.E.S.

K. THARMARATNAM

B.Sc., M.Sc., Ph.D., D.I.C., M.I.C.E.

and

A. M. MATTAR

B.Sc., M.A., Ph.D., M.Inst.Acoust., M.Inst.P.

Department of Building Science, University of Singapore

APPLIED SCIENCE PUBLISHERS LTD
LONDON

APPLIED SCIENCE PUBLISHERS LTD
RIPPLE ROAD, BARKING, ESSEX, ENGLAND

British Library Cataloguing in Publication Data
Environmental factors in the design of building
  fenestration.—
  (Architectural science series).
  1. Windows
  I. Lim, B P   II. Series
  721'.8   TH2275
ISBN 0-85334-807-3

WITH 33 TABLES AND 142 ILLUSTRATIONS
© APPLIED SCIENCE PUBLISHERS LTD 1979

Printed in Great Britain by Galliard (Printers) Ltd, Great Yarmouth

Acknowledgements

The authors extend their gratitude to all the publishers and authors who kindly gave permission to reproduce diagrams, charts and photographs in this book.

A.M.G. Arts et Metiers Graphiques, Paris: Fig. 1.22.

The Architectural Press, London: Fig. 1.21. This was published from details supplied to The Architectural Press by (A) The Pennycock Patent Glazing and Engineering Co. Ltd, and (B) Mellows and Co.

Badaloni, Jodice, Roisecco, Bulzoni Editore, Rome: Figs. 1.6, 1.7, 1.11.

British Standards Institution, London: Fig. 5.1 and Table 5.1 are reproduced by kind permission from CP3 Chapter V: Part 2: 1972, and Table 5.5 from Table 5, CP152: 1972. Complete copies may be obtained from the Institution, 2 Park Street, London W1A 2BS.

Building Research Establishment, Watford, for the use of the Daylight Protractor in Fig. 2.14.

Burkhard–Verlag Ernst Heyer, Essen: Fig. 1.1.

Mr. I. Graham, Peabody Museums, Cambridge, Massachusetts: Fig. 1.2.

Harvard University Press, Cambridge, Massachusetts: Figs. 1.12, 1.23, 1.24, 1.25, 1.26, 1.28, 1.30.

Verlag Gerd Hatje GmbH, Stuttgart: Figs. 1.27, 1.29, 1.31.

McGraw-Hill Book Company, New York: Figs. 6.3, 6.5, 6.7; from their book '*Environment Physics*' by L. L. Doelle (Copyright 1972).

Mechanical Engineering Publications Ltd, Suffolk: Figs. 1.14, 1.15, 1.16, 1.18; as reproduced from Turner, W.E.S., 'Machinery and Methods of Manufacture of Sheet Glass', *Proc. Inst. Mech. Eng. (London)*, 1930, Vol. II, pp. 1077–1127.

John Murray Ltd, London: Fig. 1.3.

Phaidon Press Ltd, Oxford: Figs. 1.8, 1.9, 1.10.

Mr. R. O. Philips, University of New South Wales, Sydney: Fig. 2.11.

Pilkington Brothers Ltd, St. Helens: Figs. 1.17, 1.19, 1.20.

Praeger Publishers, Inc., New York: Fig. 1.13.

Singapore Institute of Architects, Singapore: Chapter 3.

Sound Research Laboratories Ltd, Suffolk: Figs. 6.1, 6.2; from their book '*Practical Building Acoustics*' 1970.

Mr. S. Suthipuntha Sujarittanonta: Fig. 1.32.

Thanks are also due to all the authors for the works which are cited or quoted herein.

The authors also wish to express their appreciation to the clerical staff of the Department of Building Science and the Dean's Office, University of Singapore, for the typing and cyclostyling of the manuscript. In particular, thanks are due to Miss Tan Hooi Choo for her assistance in the drawing of the diagrams.

Last but not least, the authors are indebted to the University of Singapore for research facilities by which some of the data were obtained.

Preface

Many excellent books in building science are often written from the standpoint of a particular discipline such as lighting, acoustics, the thermal environment and the solar control of buildings. In each case the design of building elements such as fenestration, walls, and roofs are of course mentioned but only with reference to the particular discipline.

Written jointly by members of the staff of the Department of Building Science, University of Singapore, this book takes the opposite standpoint. Taking fenestration as an important building element, owing to the many difficulties in its design and construction, the authors explain the environmental factors to be considered. Particular attention has been paid to the Tropics, with which the authors are familiar. In order to avoid duplication, well-known theories are only briefly mentioned or summarised since readers may refer to standard textbooks. The aim is to present to the reader an over-view of these factors and the present state-of-the-art of control and utilisation of such factors. Reference is also made to current codes of practice.

B. P. LIM
Singapore, 1978

Contents

Chapter 1

Introduction

This chapter consists of historical notes on the design and construction of fenestration, chiefly doors and windows, from ancient times to the modern era. Reference is made to the influence of climate, the development of building materials, and the architectural style prevailing at the time.

1.1. PRE-GLASS ERA

Owing to the importance of glass as a material for windows, and its influence in architectural design, it is convenient to consider the architectural development of many regions from ancient times to the advent of glass as a distinct era.

1.1.1. *Early Beginnings*

Primitive dwellings were provided with openings for access. Whether they were constructed of mud, animal hide or sticks, an opening was necessary. Doorways of prehistoric dwellings were not unlike the entrances to caves, the earliest and most natural habitat of Man. These dwellings were mainly for shelter and for rest at night, and windows were not really necessary. Among nomadic tribes such as the American Aborigines and Mongolians, their portable *tepees* and *yurts* were only supplied with simple openings which could be covered up for privacy. Ventilation was sufficient even if a small fire were lit inside. The Eskimos' *igloos* had additional protection from the harsh climate in the form of a tunnel outside the doorway forming an airlock.

These doorways and openings persisted until the nomadic life-styles were largely replaced by agricultural settlement. The dwellings were used more often and became larger. Spaces with defined uses were added to the common area of the simple cells, and provision for ventilation became necessary. Windows were then introduced. Together with doors and doorways they formed the fenestration of the building façade, and became significant examples in the design and development of architectural style and order.

1.1.2. *Egyptian Architecture* [1.1]

Timber frames were used for doors and windows in Egyptian dwellings. As timber was precious, the frames were kept to small numbers. Similarly, windows in temples were few. The lack of openings was also due to the warm and equable climate with little storm and rain except in the Nile Delta, and massive walls of mud bricks were used to provide the necessary insulation. Sunlight through doorway and roof slits was sufficient, and there was no real need for windows. Some rooms were completely dark and windowless, such as the inner rooms of the Temple of Horus, Edfu (237–57 B.C.). For large temples, the central columns were taller than those at the side avenues so that clear storeys were provided for top lighting, a method more developed during the Gothic Period in Europe. In the Great Temple of Ammon, Kernak (Fig. 1.1), for example, pierced slabs

Fig. 1.1.   The first pylon of the Great Temple of Ammon, Kernak.

were used to cover the clear storey of the Hypostyle Hall; lightholes were occasionally also left between parapets and roofs, admitting small rays of light which created dramatic effects in the semi-dark halls with a forest of columns. Some courts were unroofed.

1.1.3. *West Asian Architecture* [1.1]

Like the Egyptians, dwellers on the alluvial plains of the Tigris and Euphrates found that stone and timber suitable for buildings were rare or unobtainable except by importation. However, clay was in abundance, and bricks were made by compressing it in moulds, then either dried in the sun or kiln-fired. Double mud-brick walls were used, and small windows were built in the inner skin just below ceiling level so as to maintain the stability of the structure. These windows did not appear on the severe external façades. Stone was used for door and window surrounds. Large openings of radiating voussoirs were erected, some with remarkable spans. For example, the Palace at Ctesiphon (Fig. 1.2) had an elliptical barrel vault with a span of 25·3 m.

Fig. 1.2. The Palace of Ctesiphon.

1.1.4. *Indian Sub-continent Architecture* [1.1]

In spite of great variations in climate, emphasis was on excluding heat from the building rather than inducing it for winter comfort. Pierced, or latticed, windows to exclude sunlight and heat were common, and the fine carving surrounding the window and door openings characterised the architectural style, accentuated by the high angle of the sun. Lattice screens were also found in northern regions such as Nepal.

1.1.5. *Chinese Architecture* [1.1]

In comparison with other styles, fenestration took on a more important rôle in the design of Ancient Chinese buildings. The reason was that the Chinese built mainly in timber, and bricks were used for in-fills or as foundations. Thus the buildings were basically of column-and-beam construction, and 'window walls' were constructed between the structural members. Consequently, both doors and windows were mostly square-headed (except for ornamental garden gates or city-wall arches), suiting the rectangular building frames. Again, the absence of glass made it necessary for lattice work to be used for security. Often rice-paper was used to afford privacy, and intricate designs made out of paper were added for decoration. Windows and doors were generally protected by eaves, and their curved outlines became the characteristic feature of Chinese architecture.

1.1.6. *Japanese Architecture* [1.1]

Like the Chinese, the Japanese also favoured column-and-beam construction in timber. Projection of roofs, also with curved eaves, protected the external walls. Window openings were filled with timber grilles and provided with wooden shutters externally, and paper in light sashes internally.

1.1.7. *Greek Architecture* [1.1]

Windows were rare in Greek-temple buildings. The entrance doors on the east front were tall, and when open, they allowed ample light to illuminate the statues. Even when closed, metal grilles in the panels of the doors would admit sufficient light for ordinary purposes. Occasionally, the temples were designed to open to the sky, such as the Temple of Apollo at Didgma, near Miletus. In other cases, light was admitted to roof spaces through holes cut in specially large tiles. Larger windows were found in public and domestic buildings. However, they were insignificant and lacked decoration.

1.1.8. *Roman Architecture*

The 'eye' of the Pantheon in Rome was perhaps the most striking example of the use of roof lighting in ancient times. This opening, 8·23 m in diameter not only reduced the weight of the dome, but also eliminated the most difficult part of construction.

While the Roman temples used the front doors to light the interior, in much the same way as did the Greeks, the Roman basilicas broke away from the Greek tradition. Used as halls of justice and commercial exchange, the nave roof was raised above that of the aisles, and windows were placed between the two levels of roof. Similarly thermaes were fitted with large windows. In domestic work metal grilles were fitted to tall doorways or hung with curtains.

The Romans also practised the splitting of alabaster into thin sheets, using them for glazing materials. (Windows made of alabaster were found in San Apollinare Church in Classe, the port city of Ravenna [1.2a].)

1.1.9. *Early Christian and Byzantine Architecture* [1.3]

Early Christian churches followed the basilica, including the use of clerestory lighting between the nave and the aisles, which also contained windows, open to the outside.

Byzantine builders followed the Roman tradition, and continued to construct small windows so as not to break up the clear surface of the massive walls. The dome of St. Sophia, Constantinople was lit by a series of small windows in its lower part, and by twelve windows grouped in the spandrel walls, north and south, under the great arches which supported the dome, while there were windows in the lower part of the domes of the exedra and of the apse. Many of the windows were small and spanned by semi-circular arches; others were more elaborate, and in the 'gynaeceum', large semi-circular headed openings were divided into six by columns of two heights, between which marble lattice screens admitted light through openings about 180-mm square, as found along the gallery. These openings were said to have been glazed [1.2b].

1.1.10. *Romanesque Architecture*

Doors and windows continued to play a minor rôle in architectural style during this period. Window tracery was not employed to any great extent in Italy. Wheel or 'rose' windows which began to emerge during this time, were rudimentary in Central Italy, while in Southern Italy and Sicily they were often made of sheets of marble and were highly elaborate. There

Fig. 1.3. The stained glass of the choir of Canterbury Cathedral.

elegantly modelled bronze doors were also characteristic of the period. In Northern Italy where the winter was more severe than that of the south, projecting porches over doorways were preferred to recessed ones.

In France, the development of flying buttresses at the intersection of ribbed vaults enabled an increase in the height of clerestories. Windows were sometimes grouped together and enclosed in a large arch. In the north, stained glass, which was more suitable to large openings, was only gradually developed. Towards the end of this period 'orders' were found around windows and doorways and served as jambs, some of which were elaborately sculptured. Some Norman examples showed in single lights, often flanked by blind arcading, although double windows with a central shaft occurred. Where there were three openings, the middle being the largest, they were grouped together. Stained glass was now used, though sparingly, in small pieces, leaded together in mosaic-like patterns. For example, the glass panels in the choir at Canterbury (1174) (Fig. 1.3), representing biblical subjects, were set in a blue or ruby ground, and framed in brilliantly-coloured scroll work. But it was not until the Gothic Period that stained glass took its rightful place in building design.

1.2. DEVELOPMENT OF GLASS

1.2.1. *Origin*

Pliny the Elder, the Roman historian, related a story of some Phoenician mariners who, when ship-wrecked on the coast of Syria, used lumps of natron to support their cooking pots on a sandy beach. They discovered that the sand melted into a stream of liquid glass in the fire. It was likely that the carbonate of soda from the natron blocks, when combined with the silica sand, acted as a flux to melt the sand into glass. Whether the story is true is difficult to be sure, but Syria has been eminent in the glass-making of the Ancient World. Glass manufacturing was in Egypt at the 18th Dynasty (1510–1349 B.C.) following the Egyptian conquest of Syria, and samples were discovered at Tel el'Amarna [1.4*a*]. It was also said that the Romans occasionally used coloured glass for making windows, since they were able to make glass large enough in size. The tinted glass was made by a primitive process of casting, the metal being poured onto a plate and then drawn with pincers. The typical composition was silica (69 parts), soda (17 parts), lime and magnesia (11 parts), and alumina, iron and manganese oxide (3 parts) [1.4*b*]. However the application could not have been significant as little glass was in fact used in large buildings. It was also uncertain whether the major buildings in Constantinople were fitted with glass windows, though glass mosaics were extensively used. In countries under Islamic influence, however, there was a long tradition of ceramic production, and glass manufacture was developed gradually. While windows were generally small, they were traditionally closed with wooden shutters, iron bars, marble grilles or plaster lights set with clear glass. Though the pieces were small and usually of poor quality, the resulting effect was usually good.

Architectural glass in the Christian World began at the conversion of Emperor Constantine. In the Church of St. Paul, near Rome (337 A.D.) there was window glass of various colours, noted by the historian Horace to be 'as brilliant as the field of flowers in the spring' [1.4*b*]. In the 8th Century the Abbot of Monkwearmonth engaged glass-workers from Gaul to fit the monastery chapel with glass. In the 11th Century the windows of the chapter house at Monte Cassino were said to have been fitted with coloured glass 'glazed with lead and fixed with iron', a technique not dissimilar to that of the stained glass windows of a later period [1.2*b*].

1.2.2. *Gothic Architecture*

The new Gothic system of buttresses freed the walls from their load-bearing function. Large areas of window were now available, and the technique of stained glass-making found a new and challenging application. The glass-blowing method of making bottles, available by the 1st Century B.C., was developed into the cylinder method and the crown method. A cylinder was blown by means of a blow-iron, cut open and then flattened out in the furnace to produce flat glass sheets. The crown method consisted of spinning the globe with sufficient velocity to enlarge the hole left by the removal of the pipe, thus converting the globe to a disc. Crown glass sheets, made chiefly in Normandy and later in England were characterised by the arcs of concentric circles. The stonework of traceried windows provided a framework for pictures of incidents in biblical history—a much needed tool for the teaching of the Christian doctrine at a time when the parishioners were by and large illiterate. The gentle flow of the stained glass not only provided light in the cathedral buildings which were now larger, but also produced the dramatic effects created by light and colour which were totally lacking in the Byzantine and Romanesque buildings.

The French technique was imported to England, and by 1240 clear and colourless window glass was available for Westminster Abbey. In 1328 the Glazier's Company was formed in London. Craftsmen such as Vitrearius and Schurterre supplied window glass to many chapels.

During the early period (12th Century), the type of drawing on the stained glass was more archaic, its colour pure and primary, and more geometric. The 'Lancet' Style, with the characteristic pointed arches and narrow windows, provided framing. In the 13th Century circular windows with wheel tracery were seen in France. The Docoratric Period (14th Century) saw the beginning of flame-like-windows, known as 'flamboyant' in France, and 'curvilinear' in Britain, sometimes known as 'second pointed'. The pattern moved from simple interlocked designs of circles and arcs, and became more web-like. The windows, too, lost the mosaic character and figures now dominated. They were more naturalistic, and used secondary colours. The late period, during the 14th and 15th Centuries, was characterised by the tendency for large windows to be divided by horizontal tracery members or transoms. This was also known as 'third pointed' and was an English development. The windows were by now much larger, with mullions running up without interruption from sill to window-head. Small lights in the upper parts framed stylised painted glass figures. They were more realistic and literal in colour.

For domestic buildings the windows became more functional. In Britain wooden shutters had not yet been completely replaced by glass, and still retained the Norman characteristics. Also, as during the Norman Period, ground floor halls had a central hearth for an open fire or brazier, and the smoke escaped by a louvre in the roof timber above, or through the small gablets at the two ends.

In Saxon buildings the windows rarely exceeded 23 cm in breadth, owing to the absence of glass, the necessity for defence, the structural limitation, and weather protection. Internal and external splays were used to increase the flow of natural light. The Tudor windows, limited by the size of glass available, had small units, divided and supported by mullions and transoms. This style also prevailed during the Elizabethan Period. In The Netherlands shutters were equally useful against driving rain.

1.2.3. *Renaissance Architecture*

1.2.3.1. *Continental development*

Windows at this period dominated the façade. The wealth of the Renaissance cities produced palaces and mansions which were not found in the Middle Ages. The arched openings with central dividing columns of the Mediaeval practice soon gave way to large bay windows, open to the floor, protected by balustrades and balconies, and set in richly sculptured classical orders. Windows were mullioned, transomed, and some contained flat or curved fan lights. Wooden shutters were occasionally found. In France, the windows grew increasingly large, and rose up into the steep roofs as dormers. In churches, too, lofty windows replaced the small openings as the drum of the dome, as in the Dome of the Invalides, and the Pantheon, Paris.

It was during this period that the technique of manufacturing plate glass was developed in France. In the middle of the 17th Century, encouraged by the need for large clear glass for mirrors and glass coaches for the nobility, plated glass was made by casting or *coulage*. The metal was poured upon frames, spread out evenly by rollers and subsequently ground and polished. Under the patronage of Louis XIV, the Manufacture Royale des Glaces de France was established in 1695 and continued until the 19th Century [1.4c].

1.2.3.2. *English development* [1.5]

In England, foreign workers continued to contribute to glass manufacture. Venetian craftsmen arrived, first in 1547 and then in 1550. License was obtained in 1567 by foreign enterprises to manufacture glass similar to that available in France (Burgundy,

Fig. 1.4. Window detail, Banqueting House, Whitehall, London.

and Lorraine). During the 17th Century glass houses were owned by monopolists such as Sir Robert Mansell, usually described as the 'father of English glass-making' [1.4d]. By the end of the century there were about 90 glass houses in England and Wales making wind glass and plate glass as well as ornamental and utility vessels. Crown glass appeared to be of better quality than broad glass by the cylinder method, and globes up to 1·5 m in diameter were made successfully [1.4e]. The first recorded use of the slide sash in England was said to be in 1685, with the replacement of windows of the Banqueting House at Whitehall (Fig. 1.4) by panes 33 × 25·4 cm.

The development in the use of glass windows in the 18th Century was towards perfection rather than innovation. The Renaissance Style of mullion-and-transom windows, now more in wood than in stone, was seen both in England and the Continent. Cast plates were produced in England by 1773. Skilled workers from France were imported and a steam engine was invented in 1789 to grind and polish the plates [1.4d]. The crown glass now measured approximately 60 × 38 cm with a slight curvature and bright surface. Its tones ranged from purple to green, chiefly owing to imperfections in manufacture. Board glass, owing to its inferior quality and uneven surface was used

Fig. 1.5.   Internal court, Hampton Court Palace.

by poorer people at lower prices [1.4*f*]. The Hampton Court Palace (Fig. 1.5) by Sir Christopher Wren was the outstanding example of this century, with a diversity of glazing sizes and large proportion of window to wall area. The accidental imperfections with glass itself added to its charm.

1.2.3.3. *Window dimensions*

The sash window and crown glass predominated together through the 18th Century, while casements were still used in small houses, sometimes alongside the sash or hidden in the attics. The size of apertures was determined by well-documented design rules which took into account sizes of rooms of classical proportions and adequacy of natural lighting. Distinction was also made between the Italian and English climate in the adaptation of classical style. For instance, Palladio, in conformity with the doctrine of Vitruvius [1.6*a*], had the following rules:

(1) Space between floor and ceiling to be divided into $3\frac{1}{2}$ parts; window to occupy 2 parts, the width to be $(1 - \frac{1}{6})$ parts.

(2) Window to be not more than $\frac{1}{4}$ width of room, and not less than $\frac{1}{5}$.

(3) Height to be $(2 + \frac{1}{6}) \times$ width of windows. Length-to-width ratio of rooms to be 5:3,

e.g., for a room 6 × 10 m, from rule (2) width to be given $4\frac{1}{2}$ parts (1 part = 1·33 m) and each window = 1 part; thus, height = $(2 + \frac{1}{6}) \times 1·33$ m = 2·88 m.

Sir Williams Chambers found that the Palladian rules did not suit the English climate as the windows so worked out were too small. He preferred the following:

$$\frac{1}{8} (\text{length} + \text{width of room}) = \text{width of window}$$

This scale is not unlike the room index which is used for evaluation of artificial lighting. The height of the window was determined by other criteria [1.6*b*].

'The window sill is placed at a proper distance from the floor, for a grown person to lean upon, the aperture will rise to within 18 in., or 2 ft. of the ceiling, and leave sufficient space above it, for the cornice of the room, and the architecture or mouldings, which surround the window'.

The external proportion of the windows followed the architectural order. For the order of two storeys, the width of the window should not exceed 3 modules, while those of single storey might be $4\frac{1}{2}$ to 5 modules. For windows containing arches they might be $\frac{2}{3}$ to $\frac{3}{7}$ of the arch in width, and the height was to be governed by the mouldings.

1.2.3.4. *Window details*

For detailed construction of sash windows Chambers noted that they were of

'wainscot, or mahogany, and sometimes of copper, or other metals. The squares of glass are proportional to the size of windows, these being commonly three in the width, and four in the height'.

He considered that sash windows were neater and more convenient than casements. Shutters should be inside the building if 'beauty is aimed at', and they were to be of the folding type and to be housed in the body of the wall.

The early sash was heavily framed and had a glazing base 5-cm wide, and was lighter and less obtrusive during the Regency Period with 1·3-cm glazing bars. In France the *croisé* windows were more popular. The transom was placed above eye level, and the lower opening was fitted with two glazed doors hinged and opening inwards. The so-called 'French windows' were suitable for openings to balconies or terraces. Louvered shutters or *volets* were added so that the windows could be fully opened, or ventilation could be maintained while the radiation from the sun was obstructed.

1.2.4. *Revival Periods*

1.2.4.1. *Development of technology*

Board glass was improved by Robert Lucas Charce and introduced to England in 1832. The cylinder was made larger, and allowed to become cold before being split by a diamond instead of iron shear. It was then reheated in a kiln and flattened

Fig. 1.6. The Crystal Palace at Sydenham.

on a bed of smooth glass instead of iron plate covered with sand.

By 1851, Robert Charce was able to supply 100 000 m² of sheet glass for the original Crystal Palace and a further 33 000 m² when it was re-erected at Sydenham (Fig. 1.6) in 1852. James Charce, brother of Robert, invented plate glass in 1839. The difficulty of grinding this sheet of glass was overcome by making the sheet lie perfectly flat by adhesion under atmospheric pressure to slates covered with leather or other suitable materials soaked in water.

James Hartley of Sunderland succeeded in 1847 in making sheets of thin cast plate by ladling metal from the founding pot directly on the casting table, and turned down to 3 mm in thickness. These sheets were suitable for skylights and glass roofing where clear, polished glass was unnecessary. They could also be fluted or impressed with patterns, and when coloured, were suitable for churches of the 'restoration' type [1.4g].

1.2.4.2. *The glasshouses*

The development of glass led to many revolutionary uses. Plant houses, using large glass windows, were built by the Dutch as early as the 17th Century [1.7a]. By the 18th Century they developed framed buildings with sloped glass roofs, and were heated. The development of cast iron made it possible for roofs of large span and of curvilinear shape to be constructed. Glass appeared to be a suitable material to form the roof in order to admit light into the building from the top instead of from the sides. As early as 1815 suggestions were made to the London Horticultural Society by Sir George MacKenzie [1.7*b*] for a greenhouse of elegant cast iron and glass quarter sphere to be built. John Claudius Loudon invented wrought-iron sash bars which could be moulded to any desirable curvature. He constructed his own house at Bayswater as a prototype to demonstrate the versatility of the method. With W. & D. Bailey, they designed and constructed numerous glasshouses for all kinds of functions, and some were very large, including conservatories and aviaries. The 30-m diameter dome built for Mrs. Beaumont at Bretton Hall in Yorkshire in 1827, was said to be the first large glass structure of its kind, until its demolition in 1832. A better-known example was the conservatory at Chatsworth, Derbyshire (1836–40, demolished in 1920) by Sir Joseph Paxton. An interesting feature of the 37-m wide double-vaulted structure was the draining of rain-water from the main vault through cast-iron columns which also acted as rain-water pipes. The water was then collected and used for irrigation.

Similar developments took place in France about the same time. Fontaine used wrought-iron to construct the glass roof of the Galerie d'Orléans, (1829–31) a part of the Palais Royal in Paris. It was destroyed in 1935. Rouhault built the greenhouse of the French Conservatory, les serres des jardins du musée d'histoire naturelle (1833), with an interior volume of 19 000 m^3, and two superimposed quarter-section barrel vaults of cast iron.

It is during this period that the 'glasshouse' effect of glass was realised if not fully understood. Additional insulation against the winter cold was provided by covering the glass with canvas, and cavity construction in some parts of roofs was used as it enclosed 'a body of air to prevent the escape of heat' [1.7*c*]. Numerous glasshouses were built all over Europe, employing ingenious devices to heat and water the plants. The success of glasshouse techniques naturally led to exhibition buildings. The Crystal Palace, London (1850–1), originally erected in Hyde Park and later moved to Sydenham (1852–4). The structure was

Fig. 1.7. Ridge and furrow, Crystal Palace, Sydenham.

a cast-iron form with a ridge-and-furrow glazing system (Fig. 1.7) developed at Chatsworth. Sashes were of wood, grooved and painted by special machinery which Paxton designed, and a 'glazing wagon' was designed to move along gutters constructed for this purpose. Again, rain-water from the huge glass roof was collected by hollow columns. The building survived 82 years until a fire in 1936 completely destroyed it.

The success of the Crystal Palace started a certain amount of 'glass-mania'. Glass was used to cover arcades, markets and gardens. Paxton envisaged glass hospitals or sanitaria where the indoor environment could be controlled by air which was warmed, purified, and rendered fit for easy respiration [1.7d] (a concept not unlike modern air-conditioning) while still allowing the sun's rays to penetrate.

The buildings for the Great Exhibitions in the 19th Century were constructed with this newly-acquired technology. The Industrial Exhibition Building in Dublin (1853) had a huge glazed skylight over the centre of the principal nave, spanned by timber arches supported by iron columns. The New York Crystal Palace built for the first World Fair in 1853 was again a huge building of iron and glass. The rivalry between cities soon gave rise to other exhibitions, many of which had halls of glass. Even when the walls were of masonry, the roofs were of iron and glass. These included the Palais de l'Industrie on the Champs Elysées for the 1855 French Universal Exhibition by Cendrier and Barrault with its 47-m wide hall; the 1862 Exhibition of the Works of Industry of all Nations, London (Fig. 1.8) dominated

Fig. 1.8.   Exhibition of the Works of Industry of all Nations, London.

by Captain Fowkes' immense glass roof, and the giant 386 × 490 m elliptical layout of the 1867 Paris Universal Exhibition (Fig. 1.9) with its seven concentric galleries. The main hall of the 1889 Paris Exhibition, the Galeries des Machines (Fig. 1.10) had a span of 115 m, the largest ever attempted at the time. The roof was of translucent white and blue glass. The structure was unfortunately dismantled in 1914.

Glass was by now accepted for roof lights. The University Museum, Oxford (1855–9) [1.12] by Benjamin Woodward (1815–61), has a quadrangle roofed with iron and glass, and fashioned in decorative 'Gothicised' Style. The National Library, Paris (1862–8) by Henri Labrouste, was another iron-framed building.

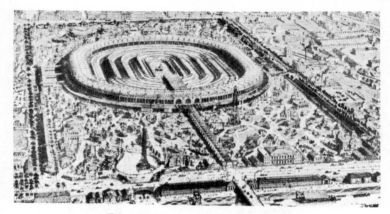

Fig. 1.9. Universal Exhibition, Paris.

Fig. 1.10. Galeries des Machines, Paris.

Its reading-room had for its roof a series of nine pendentived simple domes of terracotta, each pierced at its crown with an 'eye' providing natural top light.

The all-glass look soon spread to other commercial and residential buildings. The well-known St. Louis river front (109–

111 North First Street), built in 1849 or 1850, was a simple cast-iron structure with large glass panels. The Gardener's Warehouse, Jamaica Street, Glasgow (1855–6) by John Baird I, displayed a similar cast-iron façade with arches and large glass windows (Fig. 1.11). A number of young architects soon took up

Fig. 1.11.   The Gardener's Warehouse, Jamaica St., Glasgow.

Fig. 1.12.   Maison du Peuple, Brussels.

this theme and translated it for residential buildings. Victor Horta (1861–1947), in his Tassel House (12 rue de Turin, Brussels) of 1893 used large low windows of curved, glassed-in surface. His Maison du Peuple, Brussels, 1897 (Fig. 1.12), also displayed a curved glass and iron façade. Such departure from the classical styles was made possible by the use of large sheets of glass.

1.2.4.3. *Improvement of glazing methods* [1.4h]

The glazing method used in the 19th Century was putty glazing with wood or iron glazing bars. The expense incurred in replacing putty was the reason for the limited use of skylights until the 'patent glazing' or putty glass glazing system was developed. The early experiments included the use of 'lead came' to substitute wooden bars. The method was to fix light wooden purlins at close centres (61–76 cm), and the 'lead came' formed a joining strip between the adjacent panes. The lead strips were fixed by screws between purlins, which were grooved to receive the panes at their upper edges, and the lower edges were cut to a convex plan to encourage water to flow down the centre and away from the joining lead strips. This arrangement was suitable for roofs of steep pitch. For flatter roofs, small channels were added to the lower part of the lead strip. These channels collected small quantities of water which ran past the upper weathering webs and was conveyed to the outside of the roof. This innovation was introduced in the early 1890s, and it formed the basis of patent glazing.

Steel bars were then used to replace the closely spaced purlins which were costly. Instead of the purlins, steel 'tee'-bars, protected from corrosion by lead strips or caps which wrapped around the bars, were produced by extrusion so that they were seamless. The 'tee' section was designed so that the web stood above the surface of the glass to support planks laid over the glazing during cleaning, and the flanges curved upwards to support the glass and to form the water channels. Modifications were then made to the lead sections so that dust could be stopped by extended lead weathering wings along the edges of the panes, and the capillary attraction could be checked by additional small wings under the glass edges.

Other than this, the development of the window in the 19th Century was negligible. The sash window now had large sheet sizes such that glazing bars were eliminated. The positioning of the bars was now considered important, since in many cases there was only one horizontal bar of the double-sash window. Pepton [1.8] noted that, for the best view of the garden

'the bar ought never to be more than 1·45 cm, or less than 1·37 cm from the floor, so that a person in the middle of the room may be able to see under the bar when sitting, and over it when standing; otherwise, this bar will form an unpleasing line, crossing the sight in the exact range of the horizon, and obliging the spectator to raise or stoop his head'.

He suggested that the glass might be continued to any depth below, but not more than 76 cm from the floor, so that observers would have adequate sight of the ground outside, if the room were at ground level.

1.2.5. *The 20th Century*

1.2.5.1. *The 'glass-mania'*

The success of the glasshouses of the 19th Century led to some fanciful development in the use of glass. Advocates for glass architecture wrote with great enthusiasm. Paul Scheerbart (1863–1915) saw the use of glass as the ultimate solution of all architectural problems [1.9a]:

> *A glass house does not catch fire*
> *There is no need for a fire brigade*
> *Parasites are not nice*
> *They will never get into the glass house*
> *Combustible materials are a scandal*
> *Greater than the diamond*
> *Is the double walled glass house*

Scheerbart understood the insulating quality of air and suggested the use of double glass walls. He realised the suitability of glasshouses in temperate zones, and not in equatorial or polar regions. He pointed out the potential use of wired glass, glass bricks, and automatic doors. Scheerbart's colleague Bruno Tant

(1886–1938) designed the domed glass pavilion at Cologne for the German Werkbund Exhibition in 1914 (Fig. 1.13). The

Fig. 1.13. Glass pavilion at Cologne for the German Werkbund Exhibition.

double-glazed prismatic dome surmounted a 14-sided concrete and glass drum.

1.2.5.2. *Manufacture of glass* [1.4*i*]

Fourcault. There were also improvements in the manufacture of flat sheets of glass. The first successful process whereby sheet glass could be drawn flat, without the necessity of blowing or flattening, as found in the cylinder method, was developed by Fourcault in Belgium (Fig. 1.14). Patent was taken out in 1904, and by 1913 the process was used at Dampremy. The molten glass was forced out of a slot in a fireclay float or *débiteuse* (Fig. 1.15) which floated on the surface of the glass in a special fore-hearth or drawing chamber at the end of a tank furnace. The stream of glass was 'baited' and drawn away—in the form of a sheet by means of a series of rollers, and was cut to the required sizes.

The difficulty with the Fourcault process was the ac-

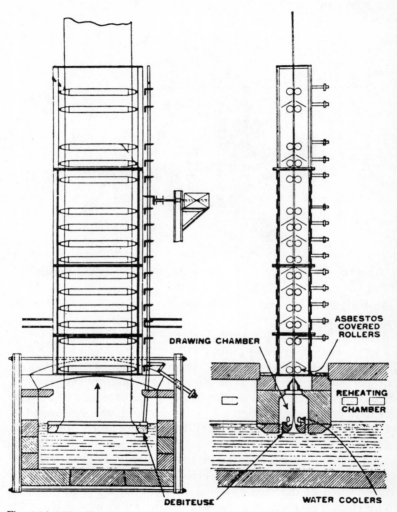

Fig. 1.14. The Fourcault process. Long and cross-sections of the Fourcault machine.

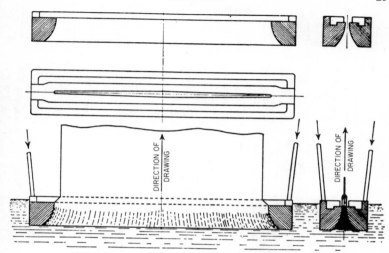

Fig. 1.15. The fireclay débiteuse Fourcault process.

cumulation of crystals of devitrified* glass. Thus the quality of the glass was poor towards the latter part of the draw, and the machine had to be stopped and the drawing chamber reheated to melt the devitrified glass every 7 or 8 days. Also marks known as 'music lines' were produced on the surface of the glass owing to the use of the fireclay slot, and were made more obvious by the devitrified glass crystals.

Libbey–Owens. Another process, patented in 1905 was the Libbey–Owens method (Fig. 1.16). Instead of the débiteuse, a pair of knurled rollers were used. The sheet, being drawn vertically by a flat iron bar as 'bait' was reheated and bent to a horizontal position. As in the Fourcault process, the sheets were cooled by water coolers and were set, then reheated over the bending roll by a gas burner before passing through an annealing lehr. While devitrification was avoided since the glass was

---

* *Devitrification.* Above a certain temperature glass may be kept in a liquid form without any change occurring, but if the temperature is lowered and maintained, crystallisation takes place. The tendency to devitrify is increased by the addition of lime. If the amount of lime is reduced, however, the weathering quality of glass is reduced.

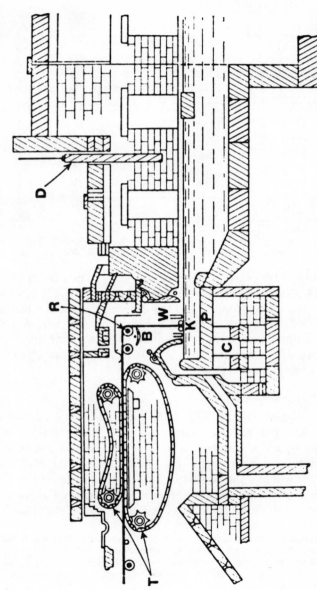

Fig. 1.16. The Colburn or Libbey–Owens process for drawing sheet glass. B, Burner; C, heating chamber; D, damper; K, knurled rollers; P, drawing pot; R, bending roller; T, tractors; W, water-cooled screens.

drawn directly from the bath instead of through a slit as in the Fourcault process, the surface of the glass was often spoilt in bending over the roller, the temperature of which had to be closely controlled and the surface carefully prepared in order to prevent damage to the surface of the glass. Together with the possibility of the accumulation of dust, the surfaces thus produced generally lacked the brilliance of the Fourcault glass.

Pittsburg. Another flat-drawing process was developed by the Pittsburg Plate Glass Company and the inherent defects of both the Fourcault and the Libbey–Owens process were avoided. The sheet was directly drawn from molten glass, but not bent to the horizontal. Thus the proper surface of the glass was preserved and devitrification was minimised. However, the drawn glass tended to 'waist' or to become narrower in width, and this was overcome by a pair of air-cooled, knurled rollers which gripped the edges of the sheet just above the level of the glass in the furnace. The edges, being gripped, were cooled to a sufficient rigidity to resist 'waisting'.

Plate glass. The development of plate glass was prompted by the need for perfectly parallel surfaces which were not readily available from sheet glass. Since 1688, plate glass had been made by casting. The molten metal was poured on a casting table and rolled out into a sheet, the thickness being regulated by narrow strips of steel laid on and along the sides of the table. After casting, the sheet was placed in a lehr, and was annealed. Grinding and polishing was done on a table of glass sheets embedded in plaster of Paris. The table was rotated, and water containing an abrasive, usually sand, was fed under runners. Grinding was done by two circular iron-shoed discs. Coarse sand was first applied, and finer grades of sand or emery were then used to obtain a perfectly flat, smooth and silky surface. After grinding, the sheet was moved to the polisher and was polished by felt pads.

Bicheroux. After the First World War new processes were developed. The Bicheroux method (Fig. 1.17) did not use the

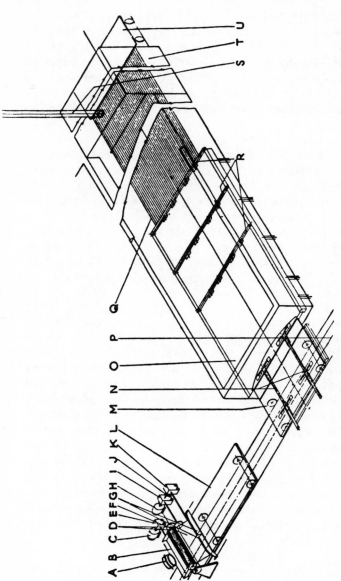

Fig. 1.17. Isometric diagram of the Bicheroux plant. A, Teeming pot; B, receiving tray; C, electric motor; D, cast-iron rollers; E, gear box for tilting rollers; F, cast-iron front tray; G, steel knives for cutting glass; H, electric motor; I, gear box for driving rollers; J, magnetic clutch; K, gear box for rack drive to table; L, cast-iron casting table No. 2; M, cast-iron casting table No. 1; N, stowing arrangement; O, gas-fired oven; P, haulage ropes; Q, travelling rails (each alternate one), intermediate rails for raising and lowering; R, internal stowing arrangement; S, chimney (pulling hot gases from oven); T, waiting room; U, cutting table.

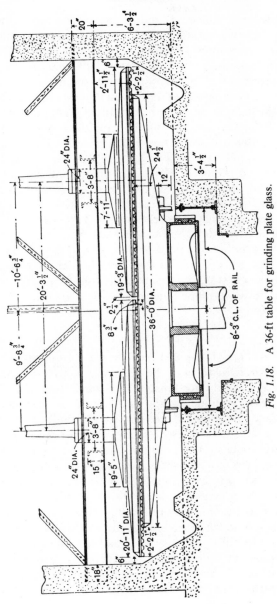

Fig. 1.18. A 36-ft table for grinding plate glass.

casting table, but rolled melted glass, producing a smoother sheet with less waves and wrinkles, reducing the amount of grinding and polishing required. The Ford Motor Company improved the process for windscreens by discharging the melted glass in a form of a stream onto two rollers from which it emerged as a continuous ribbon which was conveyed over a roller bed through an annealing lehr. In 1923, experiments were begun in England to use this method for plate glass. Pilkington Brothers Limited resolved the problem of rolling continuous sheet and provided a melting unit capable of supplying the large amount of metal required. For continuous grinding and polishing, the rough glass was laid on rectangular tables coupled together, one for grinding and the other for polishing. Later the ribbon of glass, which was cut at the lehr end and laid in separate pieces on the tables, was passed from the lehr through a continuous grinding machine which ground both sides of the ribbon simultaneously. It was then put through a twin polisher where both sides were simultaneously polished. By 1938 the process was fully developed and the whole plant was 322-m long (Fig. 1.18).

Pilkington (Figs. 1.19 and 1.20). The glass produced by the last method was thought to lack the brilliance which was found in those with a natural 'fire-finish'. Fire-finish was achieved by letting glass cool without coming into contact with solids. While the top surface could be left untouched, the under surface must be supported. In 1952 Alastair Pilkington experimented with the idea of floating glass onto a molten metal, and by 1955 Pilkington Brothers Limited embarked on a full-scale production of fire-finished glass 254-cm wide by flowing the continuous glass ribbon into a bath where it was drawn across the surface of liquid metal and became absolutely flat. Heat was applied from above and below to raise the temperature of the ribbon surfaces to achieve a 'fire-polish'. It then travelled through a cooling zone before passing over rollers. Thus the float glass was able to give high surface finish, flatness and minimised distortion. Commercial supplies were available in late 1958.

Fig. 1.19. Plate-glass furnace with twenty pots. Top, longitudinal section on centre line; bottom, sectional plan.

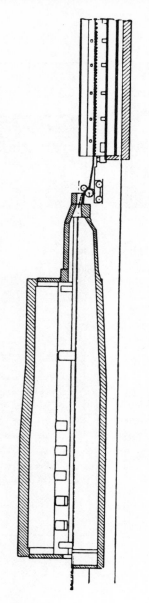
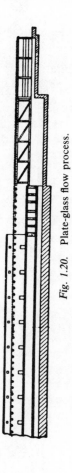

Fig. 1.20. Plate-glass flow process.

Decorative glass. Improvement was also made for decorative glass. Figured and cathedral glass made by extrusion between two rollers produced various degrees of transparency and texture by varying the surfaces of the rollers. The first double-rolling machine was introduced by Messrs. Chance Brothers in 1870. The colours were generally obtained by the addition of metallic oxides which dissolved in the metal, giving characteristic colours: blue, cobalt and copper; red, manganese and copper; green, chrome and nickel; and yellow, carbon and sulphur.

Safety glass. Safety glass was also developed—wired glass, a rolled glass into which wire mesh is inserted during the process of manufacture. The first pattern, taken out in 1855, was known as 'armoured glass'. Pilkington Brothers first made it available commercially in 1898. At first chicken netting was used, but the difference in the coefficient of expansion of the wire and the glass, and the method of twisting the wires, resulted in internal strains and led to breakage. At the turn of the century an improved wired glass with finer wire and a large square mesh of electrically welded netting was introduced. In the manufacturing process the two ribbons of glass converged and met, and the wire netting was fed between them and embedded.

1.2.5.3. *Framing and glazing methods* (Fig. 1.21)

The development of plate glass was closely followed by metal extrusion and hot-rolling processes, which gave the initial impetus to the design of metal windows. The windows were by now self-supporting and independent of the surrounding structures. Large window units could be made and fitted into the openings provided for them. The logical extension of metal windows was the development of curtain walling as a system to enclose the building with large continuous areas of glazing and panels. The curtain wall technique was necessitated by the tendency towards dry construction of components which could be made beforehand in workshops and prefabricated. The metal wall grids could be speedily erected, and glass and lightweight cladding materials were then fitted. The cladding materials were

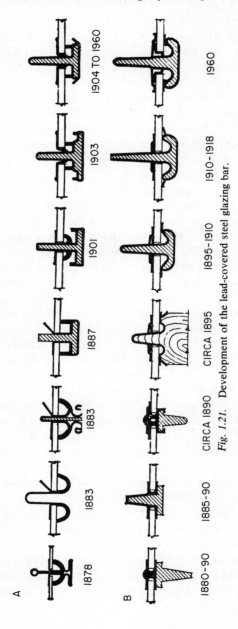

Fig. 1.21. Development of the lead-covered steel glazing bar.

Fig. 1.22. 25 Bis rue Franklin, Paris.

chosen for their weather-proofing, thermal- and sound-insulating properties. The grid was required to carry the weight of the panels and to resist wind load. Most glazing of curtain walls was by puttying or mastic-bedding with beads, and regular maintenance was required. Furthermore, leakage often occurred and new techniques were developed to overcome this problem. Neoprene (a DuPont synthetic rubber), developed by General Motors, was injection-moulded to produce a continuous one-piece gasket, without mitred or jointed corners [1.9b]. The first neoprene gaskets were installed in the company's Detroit building in 1953. The material also provided a cushion against expansion and vibration, with the life expectancy of about 25 years. Synthetic rubber was also available in various sectional shapes, and was used as spacers and glazing strips. Drained cavities were recommended by the Building Research Station, UK (1957) as a method of water disposal.

Glass was found equally adaptable to reinforced concrete

Fig. 1.23.   First Leiter Building, 280 West Monroe St., Chicago.

skeletons as to steel frames. August Perret (1874–1955), in his 25 bis rue Franklin apartments in Paris in 1903 (Fig. 1.22) expressed the reinforced concrete structure by exposing them in bare skeleton, as done for steel or cast-iron structures, and filled the spaces with large glass windows. In a similar manner Tony Garnier (born in 1869), in the project of a railway station, also resolved to have reinforced concrete frames with large glass windows. Similar application was made to masonry structures. The warehouse at 280 West Monroe Street, Chicago (Fig. 1.23), designed for Leiter in 1879 by William Le Baron Jenney (1832–1907), had brick pillars on its outer walls, and wide glass openings similar to the 'Chicago School windows' of a later date. The Manhattan building (Fig. 1.24) Dearborn Street, Chicago, completed in 1891, was fitted with large bay windows of various forms to catch all the light available to its rather narrow front. They were omitted in the upper storeys which were unobstructed. The Fair Building (Fig. 1.25), also in Chicago, completed in the same year, was another skeleton-and-large-window building, as a result of the need for a large display area required by the owners of the store. The airiness and brightness of

Fig. 1.24. Manhattan Building, Chicago.

Fig. 1.25.   The Fair Building, Chicago.

Fig. 1.26.   The Leiter Building, Van Burem St., Chicago.

the 'Chicago School' reached its height in Jenney's Leiter Building (Fig. 1.26) Van Burem Street, of 1889, and at the Reliance Building of 1894, where the architecture was dominated by the windows, which by now were large glass surfaces with much reduced projection from the skeleton surface.

1.2.5.4. *Architectural styles*

Louis Sullivan. The 'Chicago School' style was developed further by Louis Sullivan at the Carson, Pirie, Scott and Company department store (1899–1904). The 'Chicago windows', slightly elongated horizontally, were fitted with thin metal frames, and gave the horizontal movement of the façade. Later Walter Gropius, in his project for the Competition on the Tribune Tower (Fig. 1.27), Chicago, 1923, employed the 'Chi-

Fig. 1.27. Tribune Tower Project, Chicago.

cago window' with the fixed glass panel in the middle and narrow ventilating windows at the sides.

Walter Gropius. The German School also experimented with large walls. The Fagus works (Fig. 1.28) at Alfeld an der Leine, a shoelast factory completed in 1911 and designed by Walter Gropius, was dominated by plane surfaces of glass. As distinct from the Chicago School, the glass panels were supported by slender columns, and corner piers were omitted. Thus the concept of 'curtain walling' emerged. Gropius wanted the walls to be 'mere screens stretched between the upright columns of the framework to keep out rain, cold, and noise' [1.10]. The glass was said to have 'structural importance'. At the 'Fabrik' (Fig. 1.29) Gropius' model factory and office building at the Werk-

Fig. 1.28. Fagus works (a shoelast factory).

bund's Cologne Exhibition of 1914, offices were glassed from floor to ceiling, and the spiral staircases were entirely enclosed in glass, creating a new sense of space hitherto unseen. The Bauhaus Buildings (Fig. 1.30) at Dessau, 1926, influenced by Cubism, had continuous glass curtain flowing around the build-

Fig. 1.29. 'Fabrik', Cologne.

Fig. 1.30. The 'Bauhaus', Dessau. Corner of the workshop wing.

ing without apparent supports. The reinforced concrete structure from which the glass was hung was set behind the glass. The extensive transparency which permitted the interior and exterior to be seen simultaneously, gave the appearance of 'overlapping' of space and time.

Le Corbusier. The success of plate glass enabled larger and larger windows to be built without glazing bars. Le Corbusier was one of the first to visualise its potential. In *Le Corbusier* (1929–34) he described the history of architecture as the century's-old struggle for light—the struggle for the window. The evolution of the window wall 'liberated' the window from the limitation of building materials, methods of construction, and architectural style. The iron–glass buildings of the 19th Century provided the breakthrough and now a building of steel frames with glass infill was the ultimate expression of the window as an integrated part of architecture. Le Corbusier suggested that one of the walls of a room could be entirely of glass with various treatments to modify the penetration of the sun and natural lighting. He proposed a high glass wall of, say, 4·6 m, to illuminate a living-room of 10·7-m to 12.2-m deep. As the rear of the room would receive less light, he divided this portion of the room into two floors, the mezzanine floor being for bathrooms and bedrooms. In his Immeuble 'clarté' flats in Geneva, he put his idea into practice. In the block of flats where these double-floor and single-floor types were built, it was the double-floor flats which were rented out first. The windows were of flat glass, with wired glass up to sill level. At the Cité de Refuge, (1929–1933) built for the Salvation Army at 12 rue Cantagrel, Paris, the entire south front of the main building was a glass curtain wall (1000 m^2) except for the ground floor which had bays of fixed concrete and glass, known as Nevada Units, alternating with sliding plate-glass windows.

Mies van der Rohe. Mies van der Rohe first conceived the idea of glass-faced skyscrapers in his contribution to Berlin in 1919 and 1920–2. This was a design of skyscraper entirely faced with glass [1.7]. He advocated the use of glass because the structural principles of the steel members could be expressed clearly. The pavilion for the International Exhibition at Barcelona in 1929 had large dark-glass panels to reflect the pool in front, the polished marble slabs provided the enclosure of space, and the composition was made complete with the elegant statuette by George Kolbe. In the Haus Tugendhat at Brunn (1930), the free plan was enclosed at two sides by floor-to-ceiling plate glass with view of sloping gardens and the city of Brunn. After his emigration to the United States in 1938, he designed the Crown Hall, the architectural school of the Illinois Institute of Technology—a huge single space, 66-m long × 39-m wide × 6·4-m high, of glass-enclosed steel structures. For the library and administration of the same Institute, glass of size 6 × 4 m was used. At the Lake Shore Drive Apartments (1951) (Fig. 1.31) the walls were entirely of glass, framed in aluminium, and backed by standard grey curtains behind which the tenants

Fig. 1.31. Lake Shore Drive Apartments.

installed their own hangings. Grey–pink glass was used for his Joseph E. Seagram Building (Fig. 1.32) Park Avenue, New York, in collaboration with Philip Johnson. Hand-rubbed bronze was used for the mullions and spandrels. At the Bacardi Office

Fig. 1.32. The Seagram Building, New York.

Building near Mexico City, 1961, tinted glass was again used to create the opaque appearance from the outside and transparent vision from the inside. The lightness of the glass was in sharp contrast with the strong black steel vertical mullions.

Steel and glass thus generated the 'amorphous mass' [1.11]. Mies van der Rohe was able to create the smooth surfaces of his buildings and reduced them to the mere essentials by means of the simple, transparent glass sheets. Much attention was given to detail—the linkage of flat surfaces with skeleton was examined closely. His well-known expression, 'less is more', could not have been materialised without plate glass.

Chapter 2

Natural Lighting

This chapter is concerned with the quantity and quality of natural lighting, including illuminance level, colour, sky luminance, and other general lighting principles, A survey of several common methods of evaluation of illuminance is made.

2.1. INTRODUCTION

The subject of natural lighting is well documented by many able authors. The present writers therefore summarise the general design principles of natural lighting so that the reader is presented with the over-view of the methods. References to well-known theories are made and acknowledged. As the essence of this volume is on environmental factors, integration with other features of fenestration design such as overhangs and other sun-shading devices will not be mentioned here.

2.2. NATURAL LIGHTING CHARACTERISTICS

Light as received from the sky is generally known as natural lighting and sometimes termed 'daylighting'. It is not to be confused with direct sunlight which normally is more of a hindrance for visual comfort. However, the position of the sun during clear and cloudy days affects the illuminance level of interior, as the luminance from the various parts of the sky depends on the position of the sun.

The spectral composition of daylight depends on the sky conditions, as the sun's rays are scattered and absorbed in the atmosphere. Colorimetric and spectral energy distribution of the natural light is measured by the 'correlated colour tempera-

Table 2.1
Correlated colour temperature of some common radiators

Source	Correlated colour temperature (K)
Candle	1 900
Gas-filled filament lamps	2 800–3 400
Tungsten halogen lamps	3 200–3 400
Sun (depending on altitude)	4 000–5 000
Overcast sky	4 500–7 000
Ocean blue sky	10 000–100 000

ture'*. As the temperature of a radiator rises the proportion of blue to red radiation increases. Table 2.1 shows the correlated colour temperatures (CCTs) of some common sources.

Compared with the full radiator, natural lighting is deficient in the blue and ultra-violet regions of the spectrum (Fig. 2.1).

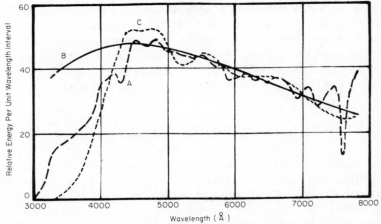

Fig. 2.1. Spectral energy distribution of daylight. (After Hopkinson *et al.* [2.5*d*]). A, Mean of 50 curves, 6400 K; B, full radiator at 6500 K; C, CIE Standard Illuminant C.

* Colour temperature is defined as the absolute temperature of the full radiator for which the ordinates of the spectral distribution curve of emission are proportional (or approximately so) in the visible region to those of the distribution curve of the radiator considered, so that both radiators have the same colour appearance or chromaticity.

While this effect does not impair visual efficiency, it is essential to supplement natural lighting with artificial lamps of similar spectral characteristics, so that there is proper colour matching. For example, most filament lamps have low colour temperatures (hence low illuminance) and would not match natural lighting. A tungsten filament lamp with a blue filter, however, is able to match the overcast sky, with a colour temperature of 6500 K. Artificial daylight fluorescent tubes of similar colour temperatures are also applicable.

The colour range of the human eye lies between 400 and 760 nm (1 nanometre (nm) = 10^{-9} metres (m)) or 0·4 to 0·76 micrometres. During normal daylight (except at twilight and dusk conditions) a photopic effect of the eye predominates and the vision is made by the cones of the retina. The maximum sensitiveness is close to 555 nm, in the yellow–green region of the spectrum. The more energy emitted at this region, the more visual sensation the eye will respond (Table 2.2).

It can be seen that over the spectrum of colour perception of the eye, natural lighting gives good distribution of power, with a

Table 2.2
Relative luminous effect of light of different wavelengths

Wavelength[a] (nm)	Relative effect	Daylight spectral power distribution[b]	Wavelength[a] (nm)	Relative effect	Daylight spectral power distribution
400(V)	0·0004	0·884	560(Y)	0·995	1·00
420(V)	0·004	0·956	580(O)	0·870	0·948
440(V)	0·023	1·04	600(OR)	0·631	0·864
460(V)	0·060	1·16	620(R)	0·381	0·896
480(B)	0·139	1·18	640(R)	0·175	0·864
500(BG)	0·323	1·08	660(R)	0·061	0·877
520(G)	0·710	1·04	680(R)	0·017	0·830
540(G)	0·954	1·01	700(R)	0·004	0·756
55(YG)	1·000	1·00	720(R)	0·001	0·681

[a]The letters in parentheses refer to the approximate colour of the radiation. V, violet; B, blue; BG, blue–green; G, green; YG, yellow–green; Y, yellow; O, orange; OR, orange–red; R, red.
[b]Daylight spectral power distributions for CCT = 6500 K, normalised at 560 nm. Henderson and Hodgkiss: experimental, mean of 54 points (Henderson, S. T., *Daylight and its Spectrum*, Adam Hilger, London, p. 181, Table 4).

slight increase near the blue region. Such even distribution is normally unavailable from a single lamp.

2.3. SKY CONDITIONS

Normally three sky conditions are considered in natural lighting design.

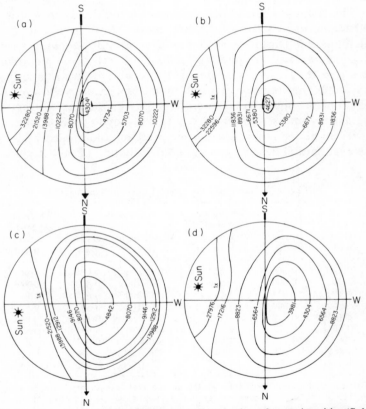

Fig. 2.2. Luminance distribution of the (clear) sky from four Asian cities (Solar altitude 15°). (a) Colombo, azimuth 103°E, February 11 fortnight; (b) Singapore azimuth 111°E, November 11 fortnight; (c) Bandung, azimuth 82°E, April 1 fortnight; (d) Taipei, azimuth 103°E, March 1 fortnight.

2.3.1. *Clear blue sky*

This is identified by a cloudless or almost cloudless sky, and the sun makes distinct shadows. Light from the sky is primarily a result of molecular scattering. The sky has high colour temperature and gives some 10^4 lux on the horizontal plane. However, its luminance is relatively low. It ranges from about 3 stilb (1 stilb = 10^4 candela/m^2) by a very bright aura of light around the sun, to about 0·1 stilb due to a deep blue path circle, which is about 90° across a great circle from the sun. The average illuminance is about 0·5 stilb.

Luminance of the clear blue cloudless sky has been well measured and documented for European cities [2.1; 2.2]. In Asia, the sky conditions were measured in several cities under the direction of Asian Regional Institute for School Building Research. The measurements taken fortnightly over one year, were for solar altitude of 15° and the azimuth ranged from 83°E to 111°E. Figure 2.2 shows the luminance distribution of the sky from four Asian cities as recorded by research teams stationed at these cities [2.3].

It can be seen that the luminance from the clear blue sky is not evenly distributed over the sky vault. Consequently the illuminance received at a particular point in a building through windows will vary, depending on the time of the day and the day

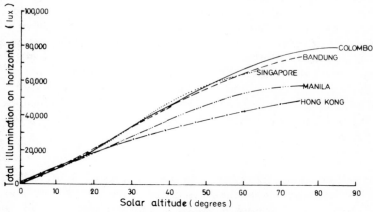

Fig. 2.3. Total illuminance on a horizontal plane.

of the year. The total illuminance on a horizontal plane, from direct sunlight and skylight for five Asian cities is shown in Fig. 2.3 [2.3].

2.3.2. *The Overcast Sky*

Illuminance from the overcast sky is found to be more constant as the sun is not visible, and there is little shadow cast by objects. The light from the sun is scattered by water vapour. The sky has lower luminance, symmetrical about the zenith, lower at the horizon than overhead. The sky luminance (L_θ) at a given angle of elevation (θ) is expressed in terms of the luminance of the sky at the zenith (L_z) and the illuminance over horizontal plane (E_h) as follows

$$L_\theta = \tfrac{1}{3} L_z (1 + 2 \sin \theta)$$
$$= \tfrac{3}{7} E_h (1 + 2 \sin \theta) \qquad (2.1)$$

Equation (2.1) gives the variation of luminance from 1 to 3 between horizon and zenith. It was first proposed by Moon and Spencer [2.4], and adopted by the Commission Internationale de l'Eclairage (CIE) in 1955 (Section 3.2, A1) as the definition of a standard CIE overcast sky. Measurements made in various stations of the world agree with the equation [2.5a; 2.6]. The relative values $\tfrac{1}{3}(1 + 2 \sin \theta)$ and $\tfrac{3}{7}(1 + 2 \sin \theta)$ for each angle of altitude may be calculated as shown in Table 2.3. It should be noted that the relationships refer purely to the *relative* luminance of different sky zones, and not to any *absolute* value.

While the distribution of luminance from the overcast sky is symmetrical about the zenith and independent of the position of the sun, the illumination as received from the overcast sky on a horizontal plane depends on the solar altitude (ϕ). An indication of the average illuminance (lux) from the overcast sky is given by [2.5b]

$$E_{av} = 215 \times \phi \qquad (2.2)$$

The unit in eqn. (2.2) has been changed from lm/ft^2 [2.5b] to lux.

The average illuminance from the overcast sky on the horizontal plane is more predictable, and the overcast sky is

Table 2.3
Relative ratios of luminance and illuminance of the
CIE overcast sky at different altitudes (θ)

Altitude (θ)	Luminance ratio[a], $\frac{1}{3}(1 + 2 \sin \theta)$	Illuminance ratio, $\frac{3}{7}(1 + 2 \sin \theta)$
0 (horizon)	0·33	0·43
5	0·39	0·50
10	0·45	0·58
15	0·50	0·65
20	0·56	0·72
25	0·62	0·79
30	0·67	0·86
35	0·72	0·92
40	0·76	0·98
42	0·78	1·00
45	0·80	1·03
50	0·84	1·08
55	0·88	1·13
60	0·91	1·17
65	0·94	1·21
70	0·96	1·23
75	0·98	1·26
80	0·99	1·27
85	0·997	1·28
90	1·00	1·29

[a]Sky luminance ratios are also known as z-factors.

more convenient to use in natural lighting design. Measurements made in many parts of the world, however, indicate that the average illuminance varies from place to place, and it is left to the particular locality to adopt its own standard of sky illuminance.

2.3.3. *The Cloudy Sky*

A cloudy sky, ranging from complete cover to complete clarity, is very common. The average illuminance of such sky condition has been shown to vary with the altitude of the sun (ϕ) measured in degrees, and is independent of the amount of cloud coverage over the wide range of cloud formation. Hopkinson, Petherbridge and Longmore [2.5c] propose that the average illuminance (E_{av}) on the horizontal plane is given by

$$E_{av} = 538\phi \qquad \text{(lux)} \tag{2.3}$$

Lynes [2.7a] also gives a similar equation

$$E_{av} = 570\phi \qquad \text{(lux)} \tag{2.4}$$

In both cases direct sunlight is excluded. Lynes further explains that the reason for the higher illumination of the cloudy sky over the overcast sky is that the brightest parts of the sky are usually the sunlit edges of white clouds, which would be hidden on a completely overcast day and absent on a cloudless day [2.7b]. The slight error of the equation immediately at sunrise or at sunset when twilight illumination is available (about 1000 lux) is not significant.

The average diffuse illuminance from the partially clear sky is measured in a number of Asian cities and is shown in Fig. 2.4 [2.3].

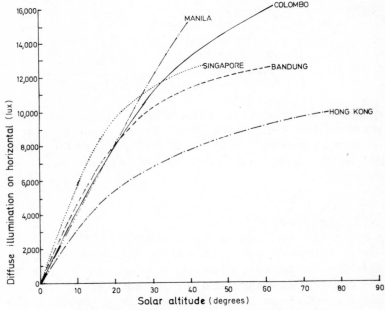

Fig. 2.4. Diffused illuminance from partially clear sky.

2.3.4. *The Uniform Sky*

The preceding paragraphs show that the luminance of the sky, and hence, the illuminance received on a horizontal plane, varies with sky conditions. The concept of a hypothetical sky condition whereby the luminance of the sky is the same irrespective of the altitude of the sun is also developed.

To simplify design procedure, the uniform sky is assumed to be a hemispherical perfect diffuser, and its luminance is numerically equal to the illuminance received on a horizontal plane under the sky without obstruction (Appendix 1). For example, if the luminance of the sky is 8000 apostilb, the illuminance received will be 8000 lux. The uniform sky may be further related to the CIE standard overcast sky by the use of the ratios in Table 2.3.

The luminance of the uniform sky may be assumed to be that of the overcast sky at $\theta = 42°$. Since the illuminance from the uniform sky is numerically equal to its luminance, the same value is used for its illuminance in lux. The following example illustrates the relationships. From eqn. (2.2), if the altitude of the sun (ϕ) is 30°, the average illuminance from an overcast sky is

$$E_{av} = 215 \times 30 = 6450 \text{ lux} \qquad (2.5a)$$

If this is taken to be the illuminance on the horizontal plane (E_h), the luminance of the overcast sky at an elevation (θ) of 42° is

$$L_\theta = 6450 \text{ apostilb} \qquad (2.5b)$$

This will also be the luminance of the uniform sky at any angle of elevation (θ).

2.4. ILLUMINANCE

2.4.1. *Service Illuminance*

Traditionally minimum or average illuminance required for a particular task or building type has been specified. The general assumption is that if a minimum level is obtained, additional

Table 2.4
Task for routine work (offices, control rooms, medium machining and assembly)

Standard service illuminance (lux)	Reflectances or contrasts	Consequences of error	Duration of task	Windows	Final service illuminance (lux)
	normal	serious +250	short −250	absent +0	max. 750
				present +0	min. 500
			normal +0	absent +0	
				present +0	
		not serious +0	short −200	absent +0	max. 500
				present +0	min. 300
			long +0	absent +0	
				present +0	

500

unusually low +250	serious +250	short −250	absent +0	max. 1000
			present +0	min. 750
		normal +0	absent +0	
			present +0	
	not serious +0	short −250	absent +0	max. 750
			present +0	min. 500
		normal +0	absent +0	
			present +0	

illuminance available from time to time will only enhance the performance of the task concerned.

The minimum illuminance concept, though in practice for many years, is now modified and is separated into 'standard' and 'final' service illuminances (in lux), as recommended by the IES Code (Interior Lighting) [2.8].

First, a standard service illuminance is suggested for a certain task. It is then modified according to the general environment, such as the reflectances and contrasts usually apparent in the performance of the task, the seriousness of errors made as a result of poor lighting, the duration of the task and the availability of windows, before a final service illuminance is arrived at. The tasks are divided into eight categories, with provision to move from a lower level to a higher one if the general environmental factors as listed above are to be satisfied. Table 2.4 shows an example for spaces such as teaching spaces and laboratories for schools, booking offices in airports, and medical consulting rooms.

From Table 2.4 it can be seen that the final illuminance may vary from 300–1000 lux. So for a classroom where error is not serious, the illuminance may be 500 lux. In a doctor's consulting room with dark-coloured walls and flooring, and where the consultation may take some time, the illuminance should be 1000 lux. Comparing with older codes [2.9] where general classrooms have been given 300 lux and consulting rooms (dark) 400 lux as minimum illuminance (with possible 50% increase) there is better adjustment to bring about good lighting requirements. For illuminance requirements the IES Code is to be consulted.

2.4.2. *Daylight Factors*

Many authors express the illuminance from the sky (excluding sunlight) in term of daylight factors. This is due to the fact that the available skylight varies considerably depending on the sky conditions (see Section 2.3). The daylight factor is defined as 'the ratio of the daylight illuminance at a point on a given plane due to the light received directly or indirectly from a sky of known or assumed luminance distributions, on a horizontal plane due to an unobstructed hemisphere of this sky' [2.10]. The use of the daylight factor not only ascertains the illuminance available for a certain task, but also maintains sufficient brightness of the interior, and corresponds with the changing luminance outdoors, so as to minimise any difficulty in visual adaptation. In general it is understood that whenever the proper daylight factor is satisfied, there will be sufficient illuminance to perform the specific tasks.

As with standard and final service illuminance levels, the IES Code 1977 [2.8] gives both the *minimum* and *average* daylight factors. The minimum daylight factors are used where the primary concern is the lighting of a task, while the average daylight factors indicate the general quality of daylighting in the spaces.

While the minimum daylight factors vary between 0·6–2·5%, most of the working spaces are given 5% for the average daylight factor, with foyers and public areas vary between 1–2%. This means that if the average daylight factor, say in the middle of the room, is about 5%, the variation of daylight factor may be from 10% near the window to the minimum of daylight factor of about 1% at the rear wall if work is to be done there. Such distribution can only be met if sufficiently large windows are provided, with the possible result of glare in certain parts of the room. On the other hand, the average illuminance may be partially provided by supplementary artificial lighting, either permanent or temporary, say on exceptionally dull days, in early morning or late afternoon.

2.4.3. *Components of Daylight Factor*

2.4.3.1. *Sky component*
The daylight factor consists of the sky component, the internally reflected component and the externally reflected component. The sky component is defined as 'the ratio of that part of the daylighting illuminance at a point on a given plane which received from a sky of assumed or known luminance distribution, to the illumination on a horizontal plane due to an unobstructed hemisphere of this sky' [2.10]. Direct sunlight is

excluded for both values of illuminance. Thus the sky component denotes the natural lighting received at a point directly from the sky.

2.4.3.2. *Internally reflected component*

Natural lighting entering a room is reflected from the surfaces of the room. After multi-reflection the illuminance received at a point is known as the internally reflected component. It is defined as 'the ratio of that part of the daylight illumination at a point on a given plane which is received from internal reflected surfaces, the sky being of assumed or known luminance distribution, to the illumination on a horizontal plane due to an unobstructed hemisphere of this sky'. Again, direct sunlight is excluded.

The general case of inter-reflection is considered as follows. An enclosure of total area A and uniform reflectance R receives certain flux. The flux which is reflected initially is f, and the flux after the second reflection is fR. Thus the total flux after multi-reflection is

$$F = f(1 + R + R^2 + \cdots) \tag{2.5}$$

From definition, the luminance of a surface (L) is given by

$$L = F/A \tag{2.6}$$

Since the expression of eqn. (2.5) is a geometric series in which R is necessarily less than unity, it follows that

$$L = f/A(1 - R) \tag{2.7}$$

It is assumed that the reflected illuminance is numerically equal to this luminance, and therefore to the right-hand term of the equation.

The Building Research Station UK, or BRS (now the Building Research Establishment) has proposed the 'split-flux principle' [2.11] for the calculation of internally reflected components. The flux entering the window is divided into two parts. The flux coming from the sky or reflected from an obstruction enters into the room below mid-height of the window, while the flux reflected from the ground enters the

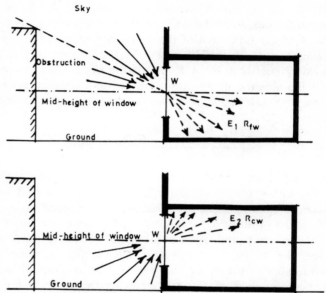

Fig. 2.5. The 'split-flux' principle for internally reflected component of daylight factor.

room above the mid-height (Fig. 2.5). Thus the first reflected flux is given by

$$f = T \cdot W(E_1 R_{fw} + E_2 R_{cw}) \tag{2.8}$$

where T is the light transmission of window glass, E_1 and E_2 are the illuminances on plane of window *above* and *below* the horizontal respectively, and R_{fw} and R_{cw} are the average reflectances of the *lower* and *upper* parts of the room, respectively, being divided by the horizontal mid-height window plane. In eqn. (2.9) A is the total room surface of ceiling, walls and floor including the windows, but excluding other surfaces, *e.g.* furniture, W is the area of all windows above or below window centre and R is the average reflectance of all surfaces including window area. The average reflectance R, R_{fw} or R_{cw} is calculated according to

$$\frac{A_w R_w + A_c R_c + A_f R_f + (A_g \times 0 \cdot 15)}{A_t} \tag{2.9}$$

where A_w, A_c, A_f and A_g are the areas, and R_w, R_c, R_f and $0 \cdot 15$ are the reflectances of the walls, ceiling, floor, and glass respectively. A_t is the total area of the surfaces concerned.

From eqn. (2.7), the average reflected illumination is found by dividing eqn. (2.8) by $A(1 - R)$. If the sky is taken to provide a total illuminance of 100 units on an unobstructed horizontal surface, the internally reflected component of the daylight factor is

$$\frac{T \times W \times (E_1 R_{fw} + E_2 R_{cw})}{A(1 - R)} \times 100\%$$

In the case of an unobstructed site and under a uniform sky, E_1 and E_2 will each be numerically equal to one-half of the luminances causing these illuminations. For a standard overcast sky E_2 is $0 \cdot 39$ times the total horizontal illumination.

If the ground luminance is assumed to be one-tenth of the average sky luminance, and any obstructing building has a luminance one-tenth of the sky which it obstructed, E_2 may be written as a factor of the flux entering the room *below* mid-height of the window

$$(0 \cdot 5 \times 0 \cdot 1) \times 100\% = 5\%$$

Hence the internally reflected component may be re-written as

$$[0 \cdot 85 \, W/A(1 - R)](CR_{fw} + 5R_{cw}) \quad (\%) \quad (2.10)$$

C is a constant, denoting the function of the flux entering the room from *above* the mid-height of the window, and includes the flux directly from the visible sky and from the surfaces of obstruction. The values for C depend on the angle of obstruction measured from the centre of the window as given in Table 2.5.

The obstruction is meant to be extended infinitely and its top outline is horizontal, while the façade of the obstruction is parallel to the window surface. The diffuse transmittance of the glass is 85%. The constant value of 5 denotes the function of flux reflected from the ground outside the window, which is assumed to have one-tenth of the mean sky luminance.

It will be appreciated that the internally reflected component

Table 2.5
Value of the constant C for different angles of obstruction

Angle of obstruction from centre of window (degree above horizontal)	C	
	overcast sky	uniform sky
0 (no obstruction)	39	50
10	35	42
20	31	35
30	25	27
40	20	21
50	14	16
60	10	11

is not uniform in side-lit rooms especially when the windows are along one side only. At a point remotest to the windows the internally reflected component is at its minimum. This minimum value is of significance since the sky component at this point is also at its minimum. The minimum value of the internally reflected component (IRC) is given by

$$\text{Average IRC } (R + 0 \cdot 25) \qquad (2.11)$$

The internally reflected component from roof lights is given by

$$KWR/A(1 - R) \qquad (\%) \qquad (2.12)$$

where W is the area of glazing (actual glass area), A and R are the total area and average reflectance expressed as a percentage of all surfaces in the room respectively (ceiling, walls, floor and windows), and K a function of the angle of obstruction from the centre of the window as shown in Table 2.6 [4.5a].

Horizontal and sloping roof lights are normally not applicable in the tropics and are omitted here. Other authorities may be consulted for further information [4.5b]. If the roof lights are of different materials from ordinary window glass, such as cast glass, wired glass, and heat-absorbing or heat-reflecting glass, correction is to be made. An approximate correction suggested by Hopkinson, Petherbridge and Longmore [4.5b] is as follows.

IRC from roof glazing = T(IRC with ordinary glass)

Table 2.6
Variation of obstruction function K for
vertically glazed roof lights

Angle of obstruction from centre of vertical roof light (degree above horizontal)	K standard CIE overcast sky
0	37
10	34
20	30
30	26
40	21
50	16
60	12
70	10
80	9

where T is the ratio of the diffuse transmittance of roof glazing to the diffuse transmittance of ordinary window glass. The values of the actual glazing used should be obtained from suppliers.

2.4.3.3. *Externally reflected component*

The externally reflected component of the daylight factor is due to the reflected light from obstructions outside windows, such as buildings. The reflected light depends on the reflectances of the surfaces of the obstructions. For example, a dark-coloured façade or trees of thick foliage will reflect less light than a light-coloured façade. However, in general, it is assumed that the luminance of an external obstruction is about one-tenth of the average sky luminance both for uniform and CIE overcast sky.

For the uniform sky, the sky luminance from any patch of the sky is the same and equals the average sky luminance. Therefore, the externally reflected component from an obstruction, designing for the uniform sky, is one-tenth of the sky component.

For the CIE standard overcast sky, the luminance of the horizon sky is only one-half that of the average sky luminance. Therefore the luminance of the obstruction is one-fifth of the patch of the sky it conceals. Accordingly, the externally reflected component from an obstruction, designing for CIE standard sky, is one-fifth of the sky component.

In practice, the obstruction is uneven as viewed from the window, and an imaginary line parallel to the horizontal plane, known as 'equivalent obstruction line', may be drawn so as to indicate the average height of the obstruction. It is drawn in such a way that there is about as much obstruction above the line as there is clear sky below. The position of the line is important, not so much for the determination of the externally reflected component but for the evaluation of the sky component.

2.5. EVALUATION OF ILLUMINANCE LEVELS

Many methods have been devised for the evaluation of illuminance levels at various reference points in a room. For expedience, relatively simple methods are presented here. It is understood that, while simplified methods yield only approximate results, they may be sufficient if building designers are interested in the initial environmental performance of the building as a whole. These methods also have the advantage that results are obtainable in a short time, and may be improved by other methods if required.

2.5.1. *The Sky Factor Method*

One of the simplest methods often used to determine the illuminance level from a uniform sky is by means of sky factor. The sky factor is in fact the sky component from a uniform sky at a point on a horizontal plane, and is defined as 'the ratio of the daylight illuminance received at a point on an horizontal plane directly through an unglazed opening, to the total illuminance on the horizontal plane due to the unobstructed hemispherical of this sky' [2.10].

In practice the reference point is considered directly under zenith at the centre of the hemispheric sky with a radius R. A cone is projected with the reference point as the apex and the hemispheric sky vault. This area of intersection is the area of the sky as 'seen' by the reference point, and is projected onto the horizontal plane by orthogonal projection. The sky factor is then re-defined as the ratio of the orthogonally projected area of an opening onto the sky vault as 'seen' from a point, to the projected area of the unobstructed sky. If the sky vault is given unit radius, the sky factor at the reference point is $1/\pi$ of the area so projected on the horizontal plane.

2.5.1.1. *Circular skylights*

Consider a building with a circular rooflight as shown in Fig. 2.6. The reference point is immediately under the centre of the

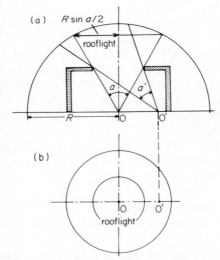

Fig. 2.6. Sky factor of a circular skylight. (a) Section and (b) plan of a circular building.

skylight. The angle (a) is subtended at the reference point, which is also the centre of the hemisphere, by the width of the skylight. The projected area of the skylight with a radius $R \sin a/2$ is $\pi(R \sin a/2)^2$. The sky factor is therefore

$$\frac{\pi R^2 (\sin a/2)^2}{\pi R^2} = \tfrac{1}{2}(1 - \cos a) \tag{2.13}$$

If the reference point is now moved to any other point on the working plane, the sky factor is also expressed by eqn. (2.13), the angle (a) being subtended at the reference point by the diameter of the skylight. This may be understood by the Sumpner-sphere method as shown in Appendix 2.

2.5.1.2. *Sky 'ring' light*

Equation (2.13) is also applicable to a 'ring' rooflight, or vertical windows of a circular building. The net sky factor is the difference of the two sky factors governed by the two angles (a) and (b) subtended at the same reference point by the outer and inner rims, respectively, of the circular sky ring, or the sill and head, respectively, of the vertical window of a circular building as follows

$$\text{Sky factor} = \tfrac{1}{2}(1 - \cos a) - \tfrac{1}{2}(1 - \cos b) = \tfrac{1}{2}(\cos b - \cos a)$$

$$(2.14)$$

Sky factor at any other reference point not immediately below the centre of the 'sky ring' or at the centre of the circular building is also found by eqn. (2.14) in a similar way (Fig. 2.7).

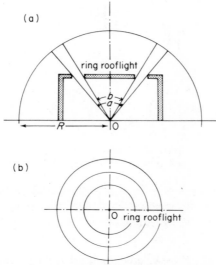

Fig. 2.7. Sky factor of a 'ring' skylight. (a) Section and (b) plan of a circular building.

2.5.1.3. *Rectilinear windows*

For windows of vertical walls of normal rectilinear rooms, the window head is projected by a plane from the reference point at the centre of the sky vault, forming a great circle on the hemisphere. The orthogonal projection of this great circle on the horizontal plane is part of an ellipse. If the vertical window is considered to be infinitely long, the projection is a complete semi-ellipse. If the horizontal plane coincides with the window sill, the projected area of the window on the horizontal plane is the difference of the areas of the projection of the sky vault, a semi-circle, and the semi-ellipse (Fig. 2.8).

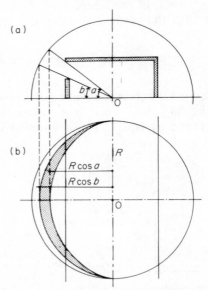

Fig. 2.8.   Sky factor of vertical windows of 'infinite' length. (a) Section and (b) plan of a building with 'infinite' length windows.

The area of the semi-ellipse is $(\pi/2)(R \times R \cos a)$ where R and $R \cos a$ are the major and minor radii, respectively. The area of the semi-circle is $\pi R^2/2$. Hence the projected area of the window is

$$(\pi/2)(R^2 - R^2 \cos a) = (\pi R^2/2)(1 - \cos a) \qquad (2.15)$$

The sky factor due to the infinitely long window with window sill on the horizontal plane is

$$\frac{\pi R^2(1 - \cos a)}{2\pi R^2} = \tfrac{1}{2}(1 - \cos a) \tag{2.16}$$

In this case the angle (a) is the same as angle (θ). For the window sill not in the vertical plane, its sky factor is the difference of the two sky factors to be governed by the projections of the window head and window sill, respectively. Hence

$$\text{sky factor} = \tfrac{1}{2}(\cos b - \cos a) \tag{2.17}$$

where b and a are the angles of elevation of the window sill and head, respectively.

Ordinary windows, of course, are not infinite in length, except in very large buildings, such as factories, where the side windows appear to be almost infinitely long to a particular reference point. The cut-off at the sides reduces the sky factor. Consider a reference point which is co-planar to the window sill of a vertical window of definite width. The window head may be projected as before, and the orthographical projection is shown in Fig. 2.9. The projected area A'B'C'D' is the difference of two sectors, PA'B' of the semi-circle and PC'D' of the semi-ellipse.

If the hemispherical sky vault has unit radius, sector PC'D' is related to sector PCD such that area PC'D' = area PCD $\times \cos \theta$. Area of sector PCD is given by $R^2h/2\pi$ sector PC'D' by $R^2h' \cos \theta/2\pi$ and area of sector PA'B' by $R^2h/2\pi$. Therefore the projected area A'B'C'D' is

$$(\text{sector PA'B'}) - (\text{sector PC'D'}) = R^2h/2\pi - R^2h' \cos \theta/2\pi$$
$$= R^2\left(\frac{h - h' \cos \theta}{2\pi}\right) \tag{2.18}$$

Putting $R = 1$, the sky factor of the window is

$$\frac{h - h' \cos \theta}{2\pi} \quad \text{or} \quad \frac{h - h' \cos \theta}{360} \tag{2.19}$$

where h and h' are expressed in degrees.

Since the sky factor of a window of apparently infinite width

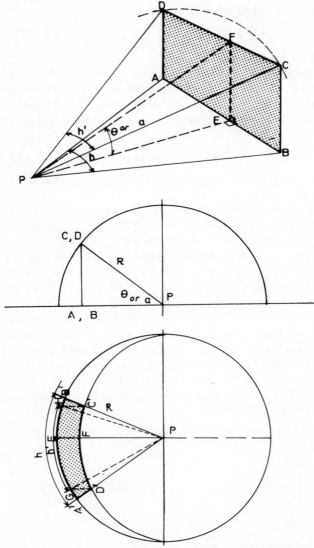

Fig. 2.9. Sky factor of vertical windows of definite width.

is $\frac{1}{2}(1 - \cos \theta)$, the ratio between these two sky factors is

$$\frac{h - h' \cos \theta}{360} \times 2/(1 - \cos \theta) = \frac{h - h' \cos \theta}{180(1 - \cos \theta)} \quad (2.20)$$

It can be seen that the correction factor depends on the angles of a, h and h'. Angle h' may be found from $\tan h' = \tan h \times \cos a$. Thus the correction factors vary with a and h. They may be computed according to the values of these angles as shown in Fig. 2.10. These factors could then be used to find

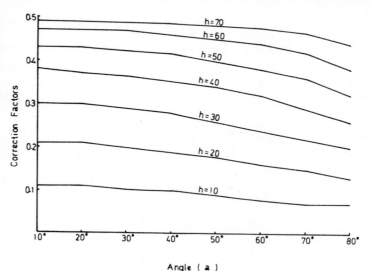

Fig. 2.10. Correction factors for window of definite width.

the sky factor (SF) of vertical windows of definite width as follows

$$SF = \tfrac{1}{2}(1 - \cos a) \times \text{correction factor} \quad (2.21)$$

Sky factor protractors are also developed for this purpose. R. O. Philips [2.12] produced a sky factor protractor with correction factors on a transparent disc on one-half of the protractor (Fig. 2.11). The expression $\frac{1}{2}(1 - \cos a)$ is plotted for the angle (a) between 0° and 90° (*i.e.* sky factor from 0 to 100%). This is

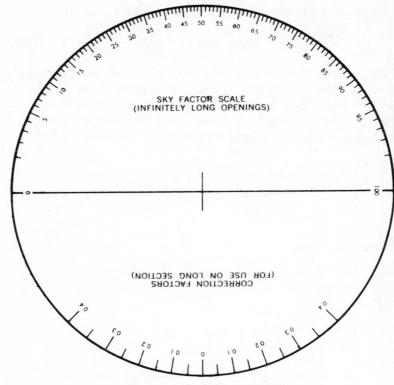

Fig. 2.11. Sky factor protractor.

suitable for round and ring skylights, and infinitely long vertical openings. On the other half of the protractor correction factors are plotted with 0 at the centre, and 0·5 at the two ends of the baseline. This means that the correction factors vary from 0 to 0·5 to each side of the normal, depending on the angular width of the window measured from the reference point to the window jamb on plan with respect to the normal; and if the window is infinitely long the correction factor will be 0·5 + 0·5 = 1.

As the sky factor concept is applicable only to the uniform sky, an approximation for the corresponding sky factor under the CIE overcast sky may be obtained by the multiplication of the illuminance ratios (Table 2.3). The application of the sky factor protractor is shown by the examples below.

Example 2.1 (Fig. 2.12a) Circular building with a round skylight.
Find the sky factor at P.

Place the protractor on one of the sight lines from P and read off the sky factor.

$$\text{sky factor} = 23 \cdot 5\% \text{ at P (uniform sky)}$$

or

$$\text{sky factor} = \tfrac{1}{2}(1 - \cos 58°) = 23 \cdot 5\%$$

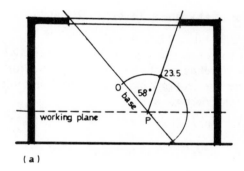

(a)

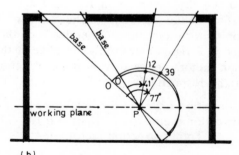

(b)

Fig. 2.12. Working examples of sky factor. See Examples 2.1 and 2.2 in text. Sections of a circular building with (a) a round rooflight and (b) a ring rooflight.

Example 2.2 (Fig. 2.12b) Circular building with a skylight in the form of a ring.

Find the sky factor at P.

Place the protractor on the outer and inner sight lines, respectively; subtract the sky factor one from the other.

sky factor of outer disc at P = 39%

or

sky factor = $\frac{1}{2}(1 - \cos 77°) = 38\cdot8\%$

sky factor of inner disc = 12% at P

or

sky factor = $\frac{1}{2}(1 - \cos 41°) = 12\%$

net sky factor of sky ring = 39 − 12 = 27% at P.

Example 2.3 (Fig. 2.13) Vertical windows.

Find the sky factor at P if the window is infinitely long.

Place the baseline of the sky factor protractor at P on the working plane (in section) parallel to the horizontal floor line. Read off the sky factor.

sky factor = 5% at P

or

sky factor = $\frac{1}{2}(1 - \cos 26°) = 5\%$

Example 2.4 (Fig. 2.13) Vertical windows.

Find the sky factor at P if the window is of limited width.

First, find the sky factor as in Example 2.3. Then find the correction factor to the 'left' and to the 'right' of P by placing the correction factor protractor on the plan such that the normal to the window is at right angles to the baseline of the protractor. The correction factors are read from the protractor to the 'left' and to the 'right' respectively.

Correction factor to the 'left' = 0·31
Correction factor to the 'right' = 0·10
Total correction factor = 0·41

net sky factor 5% × 0·41 = 2·05% (uniform sky).

For CIE overcast sky the sky factor is 2·05 × 0·64 = 1·3%.

By calculation (Fig. 2.13)

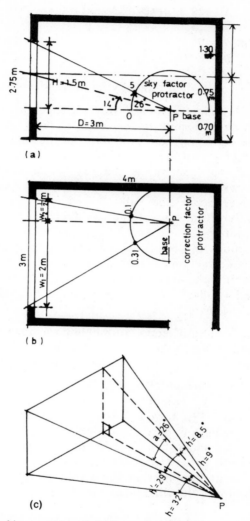

Fig. 2.13. Working examples of sky factor. See Example 2.3 in text. (a) Section and (b) plan of a rectangular building with side window; (c) angular measurement of *a*, *h* and *h'*.

To the 'left' $h = 32°$
                $h' = 29°$ sky factor $= \dfrac{h - h' \cos a}{360} = 1{\cdot}65\%$
                $a = 26°$
To the 'right' $h = 9°$ sky factor $= 0{\cdot}38\%$
                $h' = 8{\cdot}5°$
                $a = 26°$
                              total sky factor (uniform sky) $= \overline{2{\cdot}03\%}$

2.5.2. BRS Daylight Protractor* (for unglazed apertures) [2.13]

Another development is the BRS daylight protractor. It consists of a sky component protractor for long apertures, and a correction factor protractor. The sky component protractor is used in a similar manner as the sky factor protractor, the variation between sky factor and sky component being that of the illuminance ratios (see Table 2.3). The correction factors, however, differ from that of the sky factor protractor as the angle of elevation (a) is taken into consideration. The average angle (a) through the centre of the window on section is read first, and the correction factor scale is placed on the plan, and are read according to angle (a) (see Fig. 2.14). Example 2.4 may now be used to illustrate the application of the BRS daylight protractor as follows

sky component (on section of building as shown) $= 3{\cdot}2\%$
correction factor for angle (a) $= 14°$ is $0{\cdot}1 + 0{\cdot}32 = 0{\cdot}42$
net sky component $= 1{\cdot}3\%$

2.5.3. Simplified Daylight Tables [2.14]

These tables by Hopkinson, Longmore and Graham were first developed in 1958 for quick estimation of direct and indirect daylight in buildings lit by vertically glazed windows. Tables for sky components under the CIE overcast sky and for sky factors under a uniform sky are available (Tables 2.7 and 2.8). First, the heights of the window head (H) and sill (H') from the working plane, the width of the window to one side of normal W and the

---

* BRS sky component protractor No. 10 for unglazed apertures and CIE overcast sky (second series) Building Research Station, Ministry of Public Buildings and Works, Her Majesty's Stationery Office, 1967, is published here by kind permission.

perpendicular distance D from the measuring point to the window are obtained from drawings. The ratio of H/D and W/D are then worked out, and the respective sky component or sky factor can then be read from the tables.

Table 2.7 has been subsequently included in a technical report of the Illuminating Engineering Society [2.15]. Using the tables, Example 2.4 may also be re-valuated as follows:

$$H/D = 0 \cdot 5 \qquad W_1/D = 0 \cdot 66 \qquad W_2/D = 0 \cdot 17$$

(i) *For uniform sky*:

sky component to the left of observer = $1 \cdot 7\%$

sky component to the right of observer = $\underline{0 \cdot 5\%}$

$2 \cdot 2\%$

(ii) *For overcast sky*:

sky component to the left of observer = $1 \cdot 0\%$

sky component to the right of observer = $\underline{0 \cdot 3\%}$

$1 \cdot 3\%$

However, these sky components are for vertically glazed windows. If the coefficient of transmission is $0 \cdot 85$, the sky components of the unglazed apertures will be

for uniform sky = $2 \cdot 2/0 \cdot 85 = 2 \cdot 5\%$

for overcast sky = $1 \cdot 3/0 \cdot 85 = 1 \cdot 5\%$

2.5.4. *Internally Reflected Component*

The sky component only indicates the amount of daylight from the sky, to which the internally reflected component is added to complete the daylight factor, if there is no external obstruction (hence the externally reflected component may be ignored). For the room as in Example 2.4, the following conditions are assumed.

Surface reflectance of ceiling = $0 \cdot 8$

walls = $0 \cdot 5$

floors = $0 \cdot 2$

applying eqn. (2.9),

average reflectance *above* window centre, $R_{cw} = 0 \cdot 60$

below window centre, $R_{fw} = 0 \cdot 37$

all surfaces $\qquad R = 0 \cdot 48$

$A = 62 \cdot 4 \text{ m}^2$

$W = 3 \cdot 74 \text{ m}^2$

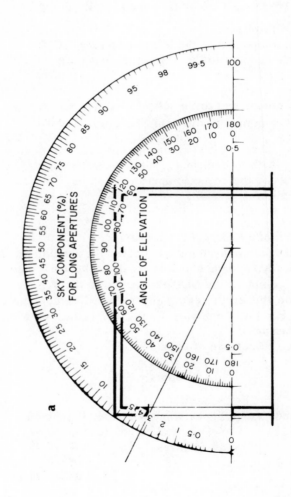

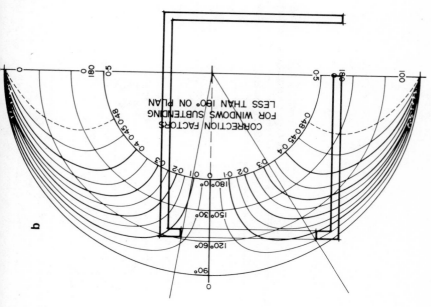

Fig. 2.14. Working examples of sky factor (BRS daylight protractor). (a) Section and (b) plan of a rectangular building with side windows.

Table 2.7

Sky components (overcast sky) for vertical glazed rectangular windows [2.14]

Ratio H/D = Height of window head above working-plane : distance from window

The left-hand column gives the ratio *distance from normal : distance from window*; the values 0 – 1·0 across the top are this ratio. (Table reproduced with the *H/D* ratio listed down the left and the *distance-from-normal* ratio across the top.)

H/D	0	0·1	0·2	0·3	0·4	0·5	0·6	0·7	0·8	0·9	1·0
0	0	0	0	0	0	0	0	0	0	0	0
0·1	0	0	0·1	0·1	0·1	0·1	0·1	0·1	0·1	0·1	0·1
0·2	0·1	0·1	0·1	0·2	0·2	0·2	0·3	0·3	0·3	0·3	0·3
0·3	0·1	0·1	0·2	0·3	0·3	0·4	0·4	0·4	0·4	0·4	0·4
0·4	0·1	0·1	0·2	0·3	0·4	0·5	0·6	0·7	0·7	0·8	0·8
0·5	0·2	0·2	0·4	0·5	0·7	0·8	1·0	1·0	1·1	1·2	1·3
0·6	0·2	0·2	0·5	0·7	1·0	1·2	1·3	1·5	1·6	1·7	1·8
0·7	0·3	0·3	0·7	1·0	1·3	1·5	1·7	1·9	2·1	2·2	2·3
0·8	0·4	0·4	0·8	1·2	1·6	1·9	2·2	2·4	2·6	2·7	2·9
0·9	0·5	0·5	1·0	1·5	1·9	2·2	2·6	2·8	3·1	3·3	3·4
1·0	0·6	0·6	1·1	1·7	2·2	2·6	3·0	3·3	3·6	3·8	4·0
1·1	0·6	0·6	1·3	1·9	2·5	3·0	3·4	3·8	4·1	4·3	4·6
1·2	0·7	0·7	1·4	2·1	2·7	3·3	3·8	4·2	4·5	4·8	5·0
1·3	0·8	0·8	1·5	2·3	2·9	3·6	4·1	4·5	4·9	5·2	5·5
1·4	0·8	0·8	1·6	2·4	3·2	3·8	4·4	4·8	5·2	5·6	5·9
1·5	0·9	0·9	1·7	2·6	3·3	4·0	4·6	5·1	5·6	5·9	6·2
1·6	0·9	0·9	1·8	2·7	3·5	4·2	4·9	5·4	5·8	6·2	6·5
1·7	0·9	0·9	1·9	2·8	3·6	4·4	5·1	5·6	6·1	6·5	6·8
1·8	1·0	1·0	1·9	2·9	3·8	4·6	5·3	5·8	6·3	6·7	7·1
1·9	1·0	1·0	2·0	3·0	3·9	4·7	5·4	6·0	6·5	6·9	7·3
2·0	1·0	1·0	2·0	3·1	4·0	4·8	5·6	6·2	6·7	7·1	7·5
2·2	1·1	1·1	2·1	3·2	4·1	5·0	5·8	6·4	7·0	7·4	7·9
2·4	1·1	1·1	2·2	3·3	4·3	5·2	6·0	6·6	7·3	7·7	8·1
2·6	1·1	1·1	2·2	3·4	4·4	5·3	6·2	6·8	7·5	7·9	8·4
2·8	1·1	1·1	2·3	3·4	4·5	5·4	6·3	7·0	7·6	8·1	8·6
3·0	1·2	1·2	2·3	3·5	4·5	5·5	6·4	7·1	7·8	8·2	8·7
3·5	1·2	1·2	2·4	3·6	4·6	5·7	6·6	7·3	8·0	8·5	9·0
4·0	1·2	1·2	2·4	3·6	4·7	5·8	6·7	7·4	8·2	8·7	9·2
5·0	1·2	1·2	2·4	3·7	4·8	5·9	6·8	7·6	8·3	8·8	9·4
∞	1·3	2·0	3·7	4·9	5·9	6·9	7·7	8·4	9·0	9·6	9·6

distance from normal : distance from window

Ratio H/D = Width of window to one side (rows) × **Angle of obstruction** (columns)

H/D	0°	6°	11°	17°	22°	27°	31°	35°	39°	42°	45°	48°	50°	52°	54°	56°	58°	60°	61°	62°	63°	66°	67°	69°	70°	72°	74°	76°	79°	90°
1·2	10·7	10·5	10·3	10·1	9·8	9·6	9·3	9·1	8·7	8·3	8·1	7·8	7·5	7·2	6·8	6·4	5·9	5·4	4·9	4·3	3·7	3·1	2·5	1·9	1·4	0·9	0·5	0·2	0·1	
1·4	11·6	11·1	10·9	10·6	10·2	10·0	9·8	9·5	9·1	8·7	8·5	8·2	7·8	7·5	7·1	6·7	6·2	5·7	5·1	4·5	3·8	3·2	2·5	1·9	1·4	0·9	0·5	0·2	0·1	
1·6	12·2	11·7	11·4	11·1	10·7	10·5	10·2	10·0	9·6	9·1	8·8	8·5	8·2	7·8	7·4	7·0	6·4	5·9	5·3	4·6	3·9	3·3	2·6	2·0	1·4	0·9	0·5	0·2	0·1	
1·8	12·6	12·3	12·0	11·8	11·3	11·1	10·7	10·4	10·0	9·5	9·2	8·8	8·5	8·1	7·6	7·2	6·6	6·0	5·4	4·7	4·0	3·3	2·6	2·0	1·4	1·0	0·5	0·2	0·1	
2·0	13·0	12·4	12·2	12·0	11·8	11·4	11·1	10·7	10·2	9·7	9·4	9·0	8·6	8·2	7·8	7·3	6·7	6·1	5·4	4·7	4·0	3·3	2·6	2·0	1·5	1·0	0·5	0·2	0·1	
2·5	13·7	13·3	12·9	12·4	12·0	11·7	11·4	11·0	10·5	9·9	9·6	9·2	8·8	8·4	7·9	7·4	6·8	6·2	5·5	4·8	4·0	3·3	2·6	2·1	1·5	1·0	0·5	0·2	0·1	
3·0	14·2	13·7	13·3	12·9	12·2	12·0	11·7	11·2	10·7	10·0	9·7	9·3	8·9	8·5	8·0	7·5	6·9	6·3	5·6	4·8	4·1	3·4	2·7	2·1	1·5	1·0	0·5	0·2	0·1	
4·0	14·5	14·0	13·5	13·2	12·3	12·2	11·8	11·3	10·8	10·1	9·8	9·4	9·0	8·6	8·0	7·5	6·9	6·3	5·6	4·9	4·1	3·4	2·7	2·1	1·5	1·0	0·5	0·2	0·1	
6·0	14·9	14·1	13·6	13·2	12·6	12·3	11·9	11·4	10·9	10·2	9·9	9·5	9·1	8·6	8·1	7·6	6·9	6·3	5·7	4·9	4·2	3·4	2·8	2·1	1·5	1·0	0·5	0·2	0·1	
∞	15·0	14·2	13·7	13·3	12·7	12·3	11·9	11·5	10·9	10·3	9·9	9·5	9·1	8·6	8·1	7·6	7·0	6·3	5·7	5·0	4·2	3·4	2·8	2·1	1·5	1·0	0·5	0·2	0·1	

National Building Studies (Special Report No. 26) *Simplified Daylight Tables.* HMSO, London, 1958. Tables 1 and 2.

Table 2.8
Sky factors (uniform sky) for vertical glazed rectangular windows [2.14]

Ratio H/D = Height of window head above working-plane : distance from window

of normal : distance from window	0	0·1	0·2	0·3	0·4	0·5	0·6	0·7	0·8	0·9	1·0	1·1	1·2	1·3	1·4	1·5	1·6	1·7	1·8	1·9	2·0	2·2	2·4	2·6	2·8	3·0	3·5	4·0	5·0	∞
0	0	0	0	0·1	0·1	0·1	0·1	0·1	0·2	0·2	0·2	0·2	0·3	0·3	0·3	0·3	0·3	0·4	0·4	0·4	0·4	0·5	0·5	0·5	0·6	0·6	0·6	0·6	0·6	0·6
0·1	0	0·1	0·1	0·2	0·2	0·3	0·3	0·3	0·4	0·5	0·5	0·6	0·6	0·7	0·8	0·8	0·9	0·9	0·9	1·0	1·0	1·0	1·0	1·1	1·1	1·2	1·2	1·2	1·3	1·3
0·2	0	0·1	0·1	0·2	0·4	0·6	0·8	1·0	1·2	1·4	1·5	1·6	1·7	1·8	1·9	2·0	2·0	2·1	2·2	2·3	2·3	2·4	2·5	2·5	2·6	2·6	2·6	2·6	2·6	2·6
0·3	0	0·1	0·2	0·3	0·6	0·9	1·2	1·4	1·6	1·9	2·1	2·2	2·4	2·5	2·7	2·8	2·9	3·0	3·0	3·1	3·2	3·3	3·4	3·5	3·5	3·6	3·7	3·7	3·8	3·9
0·4	0	0·1	0·2	0·4	0·8	1·2	1·5	1·8	2·1	2·4	2·7	2·9	3·1	3·3	3·5	3·6	3·8	3·9	4·0	4·1	4·2	4·4	4·5	4·6	4·7	4·8	4·9	4·9	5·0	5·0
0·5	0	0·1	0·3	0·5	0·9	1·4	1·8	2·2	2·6	2·9	3·2	3·5	3·8	4·0	4·2	4·4	4·5	4·7	5·0	5·0	5·1	5·3	5·4	5·6	5·7	5·7	5·8	5·9	6·0	6·1
0·6	0	0·1	0·3	0·6	1·1	1·6	2·1	2·5	3·0	3·4	3·7	4·0	4·3	4·6	4·8	5·0	5·2	5·4	5·6	5·7	5·9	6·1	6·3	6·5	6·6	6·7	6·8	6·9	7·0	7·0
0·7	0	0·1	0·3	0·7	1·2	1·7	2·3	2·8	3·3	3·7	4·1	4·5	4·8	5·0	5·3	5·6	5·8	6·0	6·2	6·4	6·6	6·8	7·0	7·2	7·3	7·4	7·6	7·8	7·9	7·9
0·8	0	0·1	0·4	0·7	1·2	1·8	2·4	3·0	3·6	4·0	4·5	4·9	5·2	5·6	5·9	6·1	6·4	6·6	6·8	7·0	7·2	7·5	7·7	7·9	8·1	8·2	8·4	8·5	8·7	8·8
0·9	0	0·1	0·4	0·8	1·3	1·9	2·6	3·2	3·8	4·3	4·8	5·2	5·6	5·9	6·3	6·6	6·9	7·1	7·4	7·6	7·8	8·2	8·4	8·6	8·8	8·9	9·1	9·2	9·4	9·5

Ratio W/D = Width of window to one side

Angle of obstruction

Ratio W/D	0°	6°	11°	17°	22°	27°	31°	35°	39°	42°	45°	48°	50°	52°	54°	56°	58°	60°	61°	62°	63°	66°	67°	69°	70°	72°	74°	76°	79°	90°
1·0		0·1	0·4	0·8	1·4	2·0	2·7	3·3	4·0	4·5	5·0	5·5	5·9	6·3	6·7	7·0	7·3	7·5	7·8	8·0	8·3	8·6	8·9	9·1	9·3	9·4	9·6	9·8	10·0	10·1
1·2		0·2	0·4	0·8	1·4	2·0	2·8	3·6	4·2	4·9	5·5	6·0	6·6	7·0	7·4	7·8	8·1	8·4	8·7	9·0	9·2	9·6	9·9	10·1	10·3	10·4	10·7	10·8	11·0	11·0
1·4		0·2	0·4	0·8	1·5	2·1	2·9	3·7	4·4	5·1	5·7	6·2	6·8	7·3	7·7	8·1	8·5	8·8	9·2	9·4	9·7	10·2	10·5	10·8	11·0	11·1	11·4	11·5	11·7	12·0
1·6		0·2	0·4	0·9	1·5	2·2	3·0	3·8	4·6	5·2	5·9	6·5	7·0	7·5	8·0	8·5	8·8	9·2	9·6	9·9	10·2	10·6	11·0	11·3	11·5	11·7	12·0	12·1	12·3	12·7
1·8		0·2	0·4	0·9	1·6	2·2	3·1	3·9	4·7	5·4	6·0	6·7	7·2	7·8	8·3	8·7	9·1	9·5	9·9	10·1	10·5	11·0	11·4	11·6	11·9	12·1	12·4	12·6	12·7	13·2
2·0		0·2	0·5	0·9	1·6	2·2	3·1	3·9	4·7	5·5	6·2	6·8	7·4	7·9	8·5	8·9	9·3	9·7	10·1	10·4	10·7	11·3	11·7	12·0	12·2	12·4	12·7	12·9	13·1	13·6
2·5		0·2	0·5	0·9	1·6	2·3	3·1	4·0	4·8	5·5	6·2	6·9	7·6	8·1	8·7	9·2	9·6	10·0	10·4	10·8	11·1	11·7	12·1	12·4	12·7	12·9	13·3	13·5	13·7	14·3
3·0		0·2	0·5	0·9	1·6	2·3	3·2	4·0	4·8	5·6	6·3	7·0	7·7	8·3	8·8	9·4	9·8	10·2	10·6	11·0	11·3	11·9	12·3	12·6	12·9	13·1	13·5	13·7	14·0	14·7
4·0		0·2	0·5	1·0	1·7	2·4	3·2	4·0	4·9	5·7	6·4	7·1	7·8	8·4	8·9	9·4	9·9	10·3	10·7	11·1	11·4	12·0	12·4	12·8	13·1	13·3	13·7	14·0	14·3	15·0
6·0		0·2	0·5	1·0	1·7	2·4	3·2	4·0	4·9	5·7	6·5	7·2	7·8	8·4	9·0	9·5	10·0	10·4	10·8	11·2	11·5	12·1	12·6	12·9	13·2	13·5	14·0	14·2	14·6	15·3
∞		0·2	0·5	1·0	1·7	2·4	3·2	4·0	4·9	5·7	6·5	7·2	7·9	8·5	9·1	9·6	10·0	10·4	10·8	11·2	11·6	12·2	12·7	13·1	13·4	13·7	14·2	14·6	15·1	15·8

National Building Studies (Special Report No. 26) *Simplified Daylight Tables*. HMSO, London, 1958. Tables 1 and 2.

Total area of room surface area of window.
Using eqn. (2.10),

$$0\cdot85\,W/A(1-R) = 0\cdot85 \times 3\cdot74/62\cdot4 \times (1-0\cdot48) = 0\cdot098$$

	uniform sky	*overcast sky*
$C \times R_{fw} = 50 \times 0\cdot37 = 18\cdot5$		$39 \times 0\cdot37 = 14\cdot4$
$5 \times R_{cw} = 5 \times 0\cdot60 = \underline{3\cdot0}$		$\underline{3\cdot0}$
Total $= 21\cdot5$		$17\cdot4$

Average internal reflected component = $2\cdot11\%$ $1\cdot71\%$

For minimum value of internally reflected component, eqn. (2.11) is used.

For uniform sky: $2\cdot11 \times (0\cdot48 + 0\cdot25) = 1\cdot54\%$.

For overcast sky: $1\cdot71 \times (0\cdot48 + 0\cdot25) = 1\cdot25\%$.

The minimum internally reflected component is added to the sky component to obtain the daylight factor at points furthest away from the window.

APPENDIX 1: ILLUMINANCE FROM THE UNIFORM SKY [2.16]

Consider a hemispherical sky of uniform luminance with a radius R, and the centroid of the hemisphere P directly under

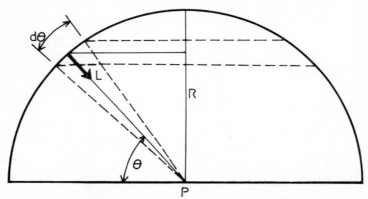

Fig. A1.1.   Illuminance from the uniform sky.

the zenith (Fig. A1.1). At an angle of elevation θ from P, an element ring of angular width $d\theta$ will have an area (A) made up of height $R\,d\theta$ and length $2\pi(R\cos\theta)$

$$A = 2\pi R^2 \cos\theta\,d\theta$$

If the luminance given by the element ring is L, then the intensity of the element (I) by definition, is

$$I = LA$$

According to the cosine law, the intensity normal to P is

$$I\cos(90-\theta)$$

or

$$I\sin\theta$$

The illuminance (dE) given by the ring to P, according to the inverse square law, is

$$dE = I\sin\theta/R^2$$

Therefore,

$$dE = \frac{L2\pi R^2 \cos\theta \cdot \sin\theta}{R^2}\,d\theta = 2\pi L \sin\theta \cdot \cos\theta\,d\theta$$

Integrating to obtain the illuminance from the whole sphere of sky

$$E = \pi L \int_0^{\pi/2} 2\sin\theta \cdot \cos\theta\,d\theta$$

$$= \pi L \left[-\frac{\cos 2\theta}{2}\right]_0^{\pi/2}$$

$$= \pi L$$

When luminance is expressed in apostilb (asb) instead of candela (cd) per square metre, 1 asb = $1/\pi$ cd $\cdot$ m^{-2}. Therefore the illuminance from the uniform sky E on a horizontal plane is numerically equal to its luminance L in apostilb.

APPENDIX 2: BASIC EQUATION OF SKY FACTOR

Consider the illumination from a small element of the sky 'seen' through an aperture from a reference point which is placed as the centre of the sky vault (Fig. A2.1). The element is

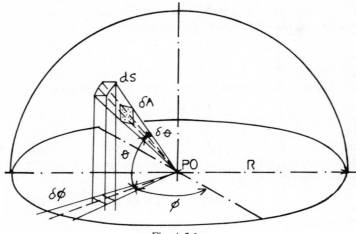

Fig. A.2.1.

defined as $d\theta\, d\phi$, where θ is the angle of elevation above the horizontal plane and ϕ is the angle of azimuth from any defined direction. The width of this element is $d\phi R \cos\theta$, since the angle ϕ is measured on the horizontal plane. The area of the element is therefore $R\, d\theta\, d\phi R \cos\theta$.

The intensity of this sky element is the product of its areas and its luminance L, which is uniform for the entire sky, that is, $LR\, d\theta\, d\phi R \cos\theta$. The illuminance at the reference point on a plane at right angles to the element is the product of its intensity and the inverse square of the distance, that is, $(LR\, d\theta\, d\phi R \cos\theta)/R^2$. Hence the illuminance received on the horizontal plane at the reference point is

$$\frac{LR\, d\theta\, d\phi R \cos\theta \cdot \cos(90° - \theta)}{R^2} = L \cos\theta \cdot \sin\theta\, d\theta\, d\phi$$

Hence for an area of sky from θ_1 to θ_2, and from ϕ_1 to ϕ_2 respectively, the illuminance will be

$$E = L \int_{\theta_1}^{\theta_2} \int_{\phi_1}^{\phi_2} \sin \theta \cdot \cos \theta \, d\theta \, d\phi.$$

The illuminance from the whole sky is numerically equal to πL (see Appendix 1). Hence the sky factor on a horizontal plane is

$$\text{Sky factor} = E/\pi L = 1/\pi \int_{\theta_1}^{\theta_2} \int_{\phi_1}^{\phi_2} \sin \theta \cdot \cos \theta \, d\theta \, d\phi.$$

Integrating between the limits 0 and θ, 0 and ϕ, the sky factor is

$$(\phi/4\pi)(1 - \cos 2\theta)$$

This is a general expression of sky factor, and is related to a patch of sky where the angles of elevation to the top and bottom of the edges of the aperture have the constant values of θ_2 and θ_1, respectively. Such a patch is formed when a rectangular aperture is curved to form part of the surface of the verticle cylinder. For instance, a circular rooflight or vertical window of a circular building are applicable. As shown in eqn. (2.13), the angles of elevation at a reference point directly under a circular skylight are symmetrical about the central axis, and the angle of azimuth is 2π. Applying the basic equation for sky factor, it becomes

$$(2\pi/4\pi)(1 - \cos 2\theta) = (1 - \cos 2\theta)/2$$

From eqn. (2.13), the angle subtended at the reference point is (a) and $\theta = \frac{1}{2}(180 - a)$. The sky factor due to the sky light then becomes

$$1 - \left(\frac{1 - \cos (180 - a)}{2} \right) = 1 - \left(\frac{1 + \cos a}{2} \right) = \frac{1}{2}(1 - \cos a)$$

which is the same as eqn. (2.13).

Now if the reference point is moved away from the centre of the skylight O to a point O' and the the angle subtended remains (a) (Fig. A2.2). From the geometry of the circle O and O' are on the arc of the same circle. Therefore O and O' are on the surface of the same sphere below the sky light (AB). According to

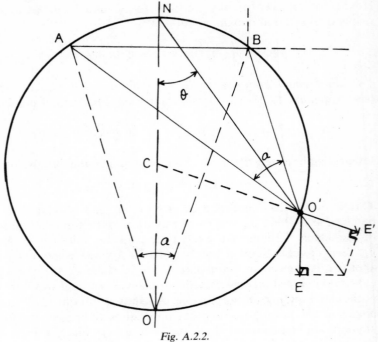

Fig. A.2.2.

Sumpner-sphere method, a small area $d\sigma$ with luminosity L gives the incident intensity of $L\,d\sigma/\pi$. At any point O′ away from the normal the intensity at an angle of incidence θ is

$$I_\theta = I_0 \cos\theta = (L\,d\sigma/\pi)\cos\theta$$

and the resulting illuminance at O′ is (Fig. A2.3)

$$E = \frac{I_\theta}{(2R\cos\theta)^2}\cos\theta = L\,d\sigma/4\pi R^2$$

The illuminance at any point O′ of the sphere is not related to the angle of incidence θ. If there are many luminous elements on the sphere, the resulting illuminance is the same at any point of the sphere. If these elements are fused together to form a disc, such as the skylight, the illuminance is the same irrespective of the position of P.

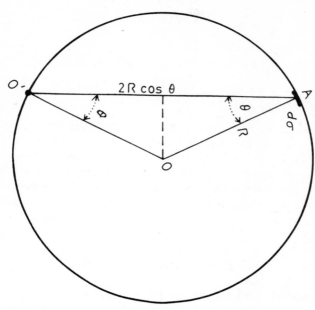

Fig. A.2.3.

It can be further proved that the vertical vector of the illuminance at O' equals the vector normal to it. As seen in Fig. A2.2, the illuminance received at O' and normal to it, OE', is along the direction of CO', the line between the centre of the sphere and O'. The vertical vector of the illuminance is OE. From plane geometry it can be seen that the extension of the line NO' bisects the angle EOE', and OE = OE'. Therefore the illuminances normal to O', and along the vertical are the same. Consequently the illuminance received on a horizontal plane at O' is the same as that at O as long as the angle subtained at O and O' by the skylight AB is the same, *viz.* angle (*a*).

Chapter 3

Solar Geometry and Sun Shading Devices

This chapter is concerned with the prediction and control of sunlight penetration through fenestration. It is written to assist in the design of sun shading devices of buildings. Throughout, emphasis is given to graphical methods using solar charts, shadow angle protractors and shadow masks. The procedure of the design and evaluation of sun shading devices are illustrated with examples.

3.1. SUN–EARTH RELATIONSHIP

In order to understand the relationship between a building and the sun a knowledge of the earth and sun relationship is essential. This can best be explained with the help of the so-called *celestial sphere*. This is an auxiliary sphere constructed with an arbitrary radius with its centre at the observer's point on the surface of the earth. The basic lines and points of location of celestial bodies (sun in our case) are indicated on its surface. Figure 3.1 shows the construction of a celestial sphere and the associated terms are explained below.

3.1.1. *Zenith and Nadir*

The diameter which is drawn parallel to the plumb-line through the centre of the earth and the observer's point 'O', intersects the sphere at 'Z' the *zenith* above the observer's head and 'n' the *nadir* below.

3.1.2. *Celestial Axis and Celestial Poles*

The diameter $P_N P_S$ which is parallel to the earth's axis is called the *celestial axis*. The points of intersection of the celestial axis with the celestial sphere P_N and P_S are called the

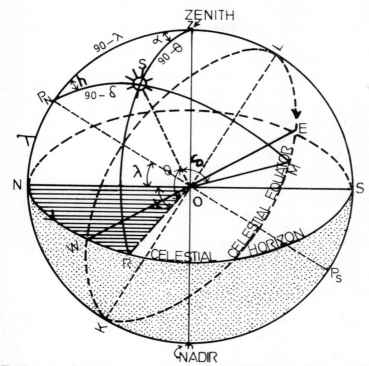

Fig. 3.1. Construction of a celestial sphere. Z, Zenith; h, hour angle (∠LP$_N$M); n, nadir; P$_N$, celestial (elevated) pole; P$_S$, celestial (depressed) pole; O, observer's position; NESWN, celestial horizon; KWLEMK, celestial equator; S, sun position; λ, latitude of the place (∠NOP$_N$); δ, declination of the sun (∠MOS); α, solar azimuth (∠NOR); θ, solar altitude (∠ROS); ZP$_N$S, spherical triangle (on celestial sphere).

celestial poles. The pole located in part above the horizon is called the elevated pole and that below the horizon, the depressed pole.

3.1.3. *Celestial Horizon*

If the celestial sphere is cut by a plane parallel to the observer's true horizon we get a great circle NESW on the surface of the sphere which is called the *celestial horizon.* This circle divides the sphere into two parts, the visible hemisphere that is above the horizon with the zenith and the invisible hemisphere that is located below the horizon with the nadir.

3.1.4. *Celestial Equator*

Intersection of the plane parallel to that of the earth's equator with the celestial sphere yields the great circle KWLEM which is known as the *celestial equator*. Its plane is perpendicular to the celestial axis. The celestial equator divides the sphere into two parts *viz.* northern and southern hemispheres. Intersections of the celestial equator with the celestial horizon yields the points E and W on the sphere.

3.1.5. *Parallels of Altitude*

Small circles on the sphere with planes parallel to the celestial horizon are called *parallels of altitude*. The one which passes through the point of the sun's position on the sphere is called the parallel of altitude of the sun.

3.1.6. *Vertical Circles*

The great circles on the celestial sphere whose planes pass through the plumb-line are called *vertical circles*. Each vertical circle passes through the points Z and n and the plane of any vertical circle is perpendicular to the plane of the horizon. The vertical circle that passes through the points E and W is called the *prime vertical* which is divided into east and west parts by the line Zn.

3.1.7. *Parallels of Declination*

The small circles of the sphere whose planes are parallel to the celestial equator are called *parallels of declination*. The one which passes through the point of the sun on the celestial sphere is called the parallel of declination of the sun.

3.1.8. *Celestial Meridians*

The great circles of the sphere whose planes pass through the celestial axis are called *celestial meridians*. The plane of every meridian is perpendicular to the plane of the celestial equator. The meridian passing through the point of the sun on the sphere is called the meridian or declination circle of the sun.

3.1.9. *Observer's Meridian*

The meridian that passes through the points Z and n is called the *observer's meridian*. This is a great circle on the surface of the sphere, the plane of which corresponds to the geographic meridian of the observer. The intersection of the plane of the horizon with the plane of the observer's meridian defines the *noon line* NS. The point closest to P_N is N and the point closest to P_S is S. The observer's meridian divides the sphere into two parts, eastern (E) and western (W). The observer's meridian is also the *principal vertical circle* that passes through all the four points Z, P_N, n and P_S and hence occupies a very definite and invariable position for the given observer.

3.1.10. *Latitude*

The plane of the celestial axis $P_N O P_S$ forms with the horizon plane an angle at the centre O, equal to the geographic latitude (λ) of the observer's place.

3.1.11. *Sun Position on the Celestial Sphere*

If we draw a line through the centre of the sphere parallel to the direction of celestial body such as the sun, we get on its surface the apparent position S^1 on the surface of the celestial sphere. The arcs ZP_N, ZS^1 and P_NS^1 form a spherical triangle whose lengths are expressed in terms of their angular distances as $90 - \lambda$; $90 - \theta$; and $90 - \delta$; respectively. By solving the spherical triangle ZP_NS^1, the sun position (as defined by its two co-ordinates, namely, solar altitude (θ) and solar azimuth (α) angles) can be determined in terms of the known parameters, *viz.* latitude (λ), declination (δ), and hour angle (h). The mathematical expressions relating these parameters are

$$\sin \theta = \sin \lambda \sin \delta + \cos \lambda \cos \delta \cos h$$
$$\cot \alpha = \cos \lambda \tan \delta \operatorname{cosec} h - \sin \lambda \cot h$$
$$\cos \alpha = \sec \theta(\cos \lambda \sin \delta - \sin \lambda \cos \delta \cos h)$$

3.1.12. *Altitude*

The *altitude* of the sun is its angular height above the observer's celestial horizon, in the vertical plane.

3.1.13. *Zenith Distance*

The *zenith distance* is the angular depression of the body from the observer's zenith and is the complement of the altitude.

3.1.14. *Azimuth*

The true bearing or *azimuth* of the sun is the angle between the plane of the observer's meridian and the plane of the great circle passing through the zenith and the sun, measured clockwise from the observer's meridian. It may also be taken as the angle measured in the horizon plane from north towards east to a point vertically under the sun. The azimuth assumes values between 0 and 360°.

3.1.15. *Hour Angle*

The *hour angle* is the angle at the celestial pole between the observer's meridian and the meridian of the sun measured westwards from the observer's meridian. Thus the sun's hour angle counts from noon (0°) and changes 15° per hour.

3.2. Solar Movement

So far the explanation of the earth and sun relationship has been discussed in general terms. Other basic facts are:

(i)   The earth which is nearly spherical in shape revolves about the sun in an elliptical orbit with the sun as one of the focii and completes one revolution in $365\frac{1}{4}$ days (annual cycle).

(ii)   The earth further rotates on its own axis making one rotation in 24 h (diurnal cycle).

(iii)   The earth's axis is tilted approximately by $23\frac{1}{2}°$ with respect to the orbital plane (ecliptic) about the sun.

(iv)   The mean distance between the earth and the sun is about 149·5 million kilometres. The actual solar distance through the year varies ±3·5% of the mean distance. Earth is nearest to the sun on the 1st January and farthest on 1st July.

The combined effect of the tilt of the earth's axis, its daily rotation about its own axis and the annual movement around the sun, produce the seasonal changes and variations in the duration of daylight and night periods which are more pronounced with the increase of latitude. The sun's declination varies continuously from $0°$ on vernal equinox day (21st March) to $+23\frac{1}{2}°$ on summer solstice day (22nd June) and back to $0°$ on autumn equinox day (23rd September) and to $-23\frac{1}{2}°$ on winter solstice day (22nd December), in a cyclic fashion. At the equinox days, both the poles are equidistant from the sun and all points on the surface of the earth have 12 h of daylight and 12 h of night. At the time of summer solstice the North Pole is inclined $23\frac{1}{2}°$ towards the sun and all points on the earth's surface north of latitude $66\frac{1}{2}°$N have full 24-h daylight while those south of latitude $66\frac{1}{2}°$ have full 24-h dark period (night). At the time of winter solstice the situation of the summer solstice is reversed. The dates of summer and winter solstice mentioned above are for northern latitudes. For southern latitudes 22nd June is the time of winter solstice and 22nd December is the time of summer solstice.

3.3. EQUATION OF TIME

Solar time is commonly used in all solar work. However, two corrections are to be made for converting the apparent solar time to clock time. These are required to take account of variations in orbital speed of the earth during the course of a year and the difference between the longitude of the locality and the longitude from which standard clock time·for the country or region is adopted. The first correction is called the equation of time which is the difference between the apparent solar time which is based on the true orbital speed and the local mean time which is based on assumed uniform orbital speed.

Equation of time = (apparent solar time − local mean time)

The equation of time varies between about $-13\frac{1}{2}$ min (22nd

February) to about $+16\frac{1}{2}$ min (1st November). The variation of the equation of time and solar declination with the day of a year is shown diagrammatically in Fig. 3.2.

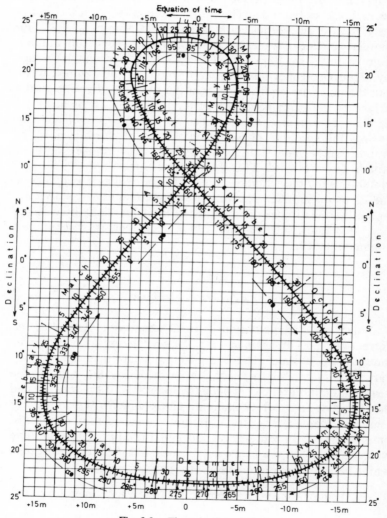

Fig. 3.2.   The equation of time.

The second correction is called the *longitude correction*. This is required to convert the standard clock time from the local mean time. An allowance at the rate of 4 min per 1° longitude is necessary. The time is *subtracted* for locations to the *east* and *added* for locations to the *west*.

3.4. APPARENT SOLAR MOVEMENT

Although it is the earth that rotates about the sun in reality, for an observer on the surface of the earth it would appear as if the sun moves on the sky vault in a specific path for any given day. For an observer at a given latitude the sun will appear to rise in an easterly direction. During the course of the time as it ascends it will appear to follow the arc of a circle which is symmetrical about the vertical plane of the observer's meridian (running north and south through the observation point). At solar noon, the sun lies on the observer's meridian it is the highest point it reaches for the day. The sun then descends, setting in a westerly direction. During the course of a year the sun is seen to travel along different but parallel paths and appears to migrate to and fro between extremely southerly and northerly positions in the sky and on the horizon. For example, at the equinoxes the sun rises due east and sets due west. Between the spring equinox, and the summer solstice, it rises and sets little further north of east and west respectively, the extreme position is reached at the solstice. Thereafter it gradually returns until the autumnal equinox is reached. Then until the winter solstice, the sun rises and sets a little further south-east and south-west each day until the extreme positions are reached. The reverse occurs until the sun returns to its equinox positions. This annual cycle repeats itself.

The basic pattern of the daily path of the sun is true for all latitudes but the angle of the plane of the path relative to the plane running vertically and east–west is equal to the latitude. The noon altitudes of the sun for any place are obtained by

$(90 - \lambda + \delta)$ for summer days and $(90 - \lambda - \delta)$ for winter days

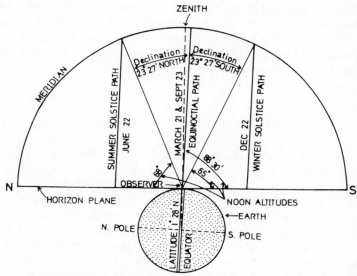

Fig. 3.3.   Construction of basic sun path diagram for latitude 1°28′N.

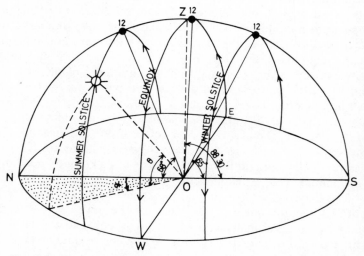

Fig. 3.4.   Sun paths for latitude 1°28′N (on equinox and solstice days).

The noon azimuth for all days will either be 0 or 180° (north or south). Altitudes and azimuths for any time of the day of the year can be calculated using the formulae given in the earlier section. A 24-h summer solstice day occurs at latitude $66\frac{1}{2}°$N. At the North Pole sun paths are parallel with the ground plane. The apparent sun paths for Singapore latitude (1°28'N) in section and isometric view are illustrated in Figs. 3.3 and 3.4, respectively.

3.5. SUN PATH DIAGRAM (SOLAR CHART)

A solar chart or sun path diagram is a plane representation of the celestial sphere and the apparent solar paths across it, obtained by a suitable projection such as stereographic, orthographic or equidistant projections. The main differences between these types of projections lie in the altitude scales and the nature of the curved lines. The azimuthal lines are radial lines in all the types of projections. Stereographic projection which is widely used has a distinct advantage in so far as the sun path lines and hour lines are arcs of circles and hence easier to draw them. However in this projection the distance between the altitude circles diminishes as the altitude increases. This is not a great disadvantage. A solar chart of stereographic projection for the latitude of Singapore (1°28'N) is shown in Fig. 3.5. The radius of the diagram is taken as 76·2 mm (3 in.). The concentric circles represent the angles of altitudes at 5° intervals. The centre of the diagram represents the zenith and the outermost circle the horizon. The radial graduations marked on the circumference represent the azimuthal angles measured from true north. The sun path for days of selected declination values (0, ±5, ±10, ±15, ±20 and ±$23\frac{1}{2}$°) are represented by a series of curved lines running from easterly to westerly horizons. These paths are crossed by hour lines which are also curved lines, forming a grid. The point where the time line cuts the sun path line represents the sun position for that time on that particular day. The sun's altitude and azimuth angles may then be read from the circular and radial scales provided. The sun positions for other desired dates than those given in the chart can be found by interpolation. It is worth

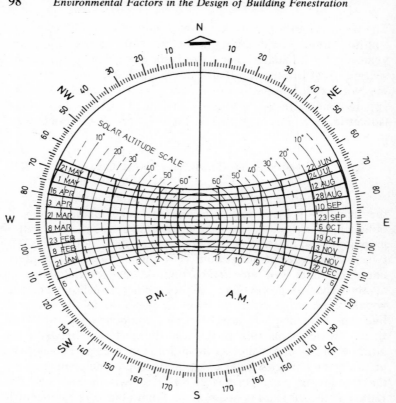

Fig. 3.5.   Solar chart for Singapore (latitude 1°28′N) (stereographic projection).

noting that solar charts vary according to latitude only and locations of the same solar chart. For example, the sun's altitude and azimuths at 9 a.m. (solar time) on the 21st May at Singapore are 42° and 63° (east of north) respectively.

As mentioned earlier, the path of the sun across the sky on any day is a circle on the stereographic projection whose radius (R_s) and position of its centre (D_s) depend on the latitude of the place for which the diagram is drawn and the declination of the day. These and the radius and the distance of hour circles (R_h and D_h^1, D_h^2) can be computed from the equations given below

$$R_s = R \cos \delta/(\sin \lambda + \sin \delta)$$
$$D_s = R \cos \lambda/(\sin \lambda + \sin \delta)$$

and

$$R_h = R \sec \lambda \operatorname{cosec} h$$
$$D_{h^1} = R \tan \lambda$$
$$D_{h^2} = \pm R \sec \lambda \cot h$$

where δ = declination, λ = latitude, h = hour angle (noon = $0°$), and R = radius of the stereographic projection of the horizon circle. Most diagrams and overlays available have $R = 76\cdot2$ mm (3 in.).

From a solar chart we can also obtain the number of daylight hours (photo-period) for any day of the year at that latitude.

3.6. BUILDING AND SUN RELATIONSHIP

For building applications, the determination of the sun position in terms of altitude and azimuth alone is not sufficient. The extent of sunlight penetration into a building, shadows cast by overhangs and other projections fixed to the walls, and the extent of shading by adjoining buildings and other obstructions, depend on the angles at which the sun's rays fall on building surfaces. The solar angles with respect to a building surface will not only depend on the sun's position but also on the orientation of the wall or sloped roof. For this purpose the relation between the solar altitude, azimuth and the aspect angle (orientation) of the surface and the shadow angles (vertical and horizontal) are to be established. These angles are explained geometrically in Fig. 3.6.

3.6.1. *Solar Angles with Respect to a Building Surface*

3.6.1.1. *Vertical shadow angle (VSA)*
This is defined as the angular difference between a horizontal plane and a plane tilted about a horizontal plane of the vertical

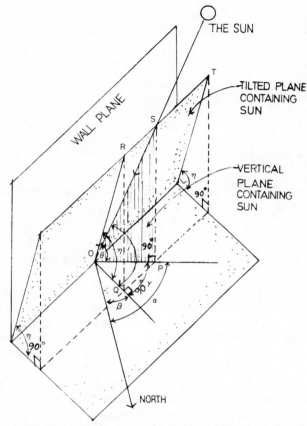

Fig. 3.6. Sun angles with respect to a building wall surface. ∠SOP = θ, solar altitude angle (vertical plane); ∠NOP = α, solar azimuth angle (horizontal plane); ∠SOQ = i, solar incidence angle (tilted plane); ∠QOR = η, vertical shadow angle (VSA) (tilted plane); ∠QOP = γ, horizontal shadow angle (HSA) (horizontal plane); ∠NOQ = β, wall aspect angle (orientation) (horizontal plane).

surface until it includes the sun. In Fig. 3.6 it is shown by the angle QOR.

3.6.1.2. *Horizontal shadow angle (HSA)*

This is defined as the angle in plan between the normal to the surface and the direction of the sun. In Fig. 3.6 it is shown by the angle QOP.

3.6.1.3. *Orientation or aspect angle*

The orientation of the surface is determined by the angle in plan, between the true north and normal to the surface. This is shown in Fig. 3.6 by the angle NOQ and the symbol used is 'β'.

3.6.1.4. *Angle of incidence*

In Fig. 3.6 the angle SOQ *i.e.* the angle between the normal to the surface OQ and the sun's ray SO, gives the angles of incidence. The symbol used is 'i'. Angle SOP in the vertical plane is the solar altitude (θ) and the angle NOP in horizontal plane, is the solar azimuth (α).

The mathematical expressions for vertical and horizontal shadow angles in terms of solar altitude, azimuth and orientation of the surface are

$$\tan(VSA) = \tan \theta / \cos \gamma$$

and

$$HSA = (\alpha - \beta)$$

These angles are illustrated in Fig. 3.6.

3.7. SHADOW ANGLE PROTRACTOR

Shadow angles can also be determined directly with the aid of a special protractor called *shadow angle protractor*. This is used as an overlay drawn on a transparent material, to the same scale as the solar chart on which it is to be used. Figure 3.7 illustrates such a shadow angle protractor. The baseline represents a vertical surface and the semi-circle represents the 0° vertical shadow angle. The rest of the curved lines represent vertical shadow angles at 5° intervals. The radial lines correspond to horizontal shadow angles. When the horizontal shadow angle is 0°, the vertical shadow angles will be equal to solar altitude. So the scale of VSA at the centre line (0° HSA) of the protractor coincides exactly with the scale of solar altitudes on the solar chart. The curved lines of VSA's are all arcs of circles, whose centres are at a distance of $R \tan(VSA)$, from the

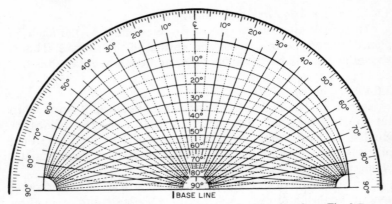

Fig. 3.7.   Shadow angle protractor (to be used with solar chart, Fig. 3.5).

baseline along the 0° HSA and with a radius of $R \sec(\text{VSA})$ (R = radius of the sun path diagram).

For example, let us assume that we are interested to find the shadow angles for a south-east wall on the 8th February at 9 a.m. The shadow angle protractor should be placed on the solar chart such that the baseline of the protractor coincides with NE–SW line and the central line of the protractor coincides with the SE on the solar chart. The time and day, for which the shadow angles are to be found, fix the sun position on the solar chart. The curved and the radial lines of the protractor that pass through the point of sun positions give the vertical and horizontal shadow angles as 45° and 25°, respectively. If the point lies in between the graduated lines of the protractor interpolated values are to be taken. The intersection of the baseline with the sun path grid would provide the information on the sun arrival and departure times on different days for that oriented wall, thus the possible sunshine hours are also obtained from the protractor. Another advantage of the shadow angles is that they could be used with conventional plans, sections and elevations for the graphical determination of sunlight penetration into buildings through openings, shadows cast by projections and nearby buildings.

3.8. MAGNETIC VARIATION

From the previous section it can be seen that the shadow angles depend on the orientation of the building surface. In solar charts the true geographical north is taken as the reference point for finding the bearing angles. However it is common to find the orientation by a magnetic compass which gives the magnetic north. The magnetic north deviates by several degrees from the 'true north' for many places. This deviation between the true and magnetic north is called magnetic variation. Figure 3.8 shows

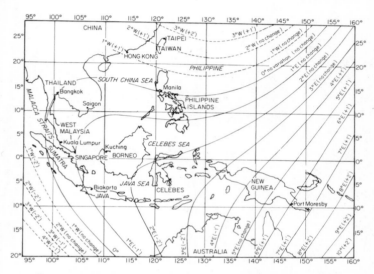

Fig. 3.8. Magnetic variation contours for South-East Asia.

the magnetic variation contours for the south-east region. From this we may note that at Singapore the magnetic north varies by 1°E from true north. Thus for example a building face oriented to 30°E of north by compass is actually facing 31°E of 'true' north and for the purposes of solar angle determination we should take its orientation as 31° east of north.

3.9. SHADOW ANGLE PROTRACTOR APPLICATIONS

3.9.1. *Shadow Casting*

Shadows cast by buildings or other obstructions can be constructed once the shadow angles for those faces that will cast the shadows are determined with the aid of the shadow angle protractor. Figure 3.9 illustrates the procedure for con-

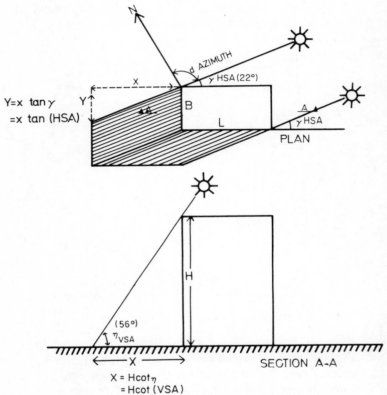

Fig. 3.9. Construction of shadow cast by a building.

structing the shadows cast by a building. The width of the shadow cast (X) will depend on the height of the building and the vertical shadow angle VSA. This will be equal to

$H \cot(VSA)$. The direction of the shadow will depend on the horizontal shadow angle (HSA). $Y = X \tan(HSA)$. This fixes one corner point. By drawing HSA lines from all other corners the complete shadow cast diagram of the building can be determined. The procedure is basically the same whichever face is used, the only difference being the section used.

3.9.2. *Shadow Cast by Projections Fixed to a Wall*

The procedure for a graphical construction of the shadows cast by horizontal vertical, combined horizontal and vertical, and overhangs of sloped roof, on the glazed area of a wall are illustrated with the aid of conventional front elevation, side elevation and plan diagrams in Fig. 3.10. All the examples are for Singapore (1°28′N).

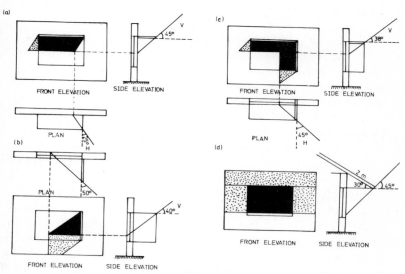

Fig. 3.10. Shadow casting by projections.

(a)   Shadow cast by a horizontal projection of 1-m width fixed at the window top, at 9 a.m. (solar time) on the 8th February, for south-east orientation. For this condition the VSA = 45° and HSA = 25°.

(b)   Shadow cast by a vertical louvre of 1·5-m width fixed on the left side of the window, at 8 a.m. on April 3, for the same orientation (*i.e.* south-east), The VSA and HSA for this situation are 40° and 50°, respectively.

(c)   Shadow cast by a combination of a horizontal vertical louvre, both of 1-m width, at 8 a.m. on the 21st March for the same orientation (south-east). The corresponding VSA and HSA are 38° and 45°, respectively.

(d)   Shadow cast by an overhang of a sloped roof of 30° inclination projected out of 2-m length from the wall, at 9 a.m. on the 3rd November for the same wall (south-east). The vertical shadow angle (VSA) is 45° and the horizontal shadow angle (HSA) is 25°.

In Figs. 3.10 and 3.11 the darkened portions indicate the shaded area of the window and dotted portion indicate the wall area under shade. The rest of the portion is exposed to the sun.

3.9.3. *Design of Shading Devices*

In the above examples we dealt with louvres of given width and the shadows cast by them. The problem of designing a shading device is the reverse case. For this the designer should determine the dimension of the shading devices, vertical, horizontal, inclined, or egg-crate type louvre systems that would completely (100%) or 50%, shade a window at specified times. The procedure is explained through examples in Fig. 3.11.

What should be the dimensions of a horizontal projection fixed at 0·3 m above the top level of a window, that would completely shade the window at 3 p.m. on the 12th August, for a west wall? The VSA and HSA for this situation are 45° and 20° respectively. Draw a line of 45° from the bottom level (sill) of the window and extend the horizontal projection from the level at which it is supposed to be fixed 0·3 m above the top of window till it meets the 45° line. This gives the width of the horizontal projection that would cast a vertical shadow down to the bottom level of the window for the required time. However it can be seen that if the length of the projection is exactly the same as the window width, there will be a triangular portion of the window left unshaded. In order to cover this area also, the

(a)

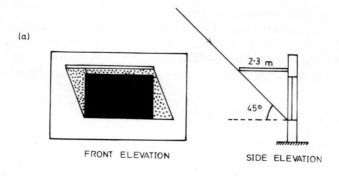

FRONT ELEVATION   SIDE ELEVATION

(b)

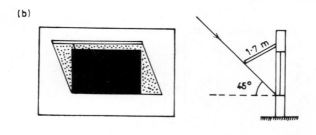

FRONT ELEVATION   SIDE ELEVATION

Fig. 3.11. Design of shading devices.

projection is to be extended beyond the width of the window. This additional length can be obtained from HSA and the width of the projection.

What should be the length of an inclined louvre which makes an angle of 60° with the wall for the above case. In this case the shadow angles will be the same as in Fig. 3.11a (see Fig. 3.11b). As in the previous case, the inclined projection is extended till it meets the 45° (VSA) line. Measure the length of the inclined line. This gives the width of the inclined louvre that would cast a vertical shadow down to the bottom level of the window. This louvre has to be extended beyond the width of the window in order to cover the triangular area.

3.9.4. *Sunlight Penetration into a Room*

It is of interest to determine the areas of sunlight penetration into a room through glazings with or without shading devices. The procedure for obtaining this information is illustrated in Fig. 3.12. The VSAs are drawn on the section at the front edge of the

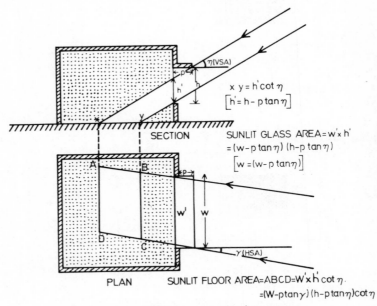

Fig. 3.12.   Sunlight penetration into a room.

horizontal projection and inner edge of sill and projected onto the floor. The space between two parallel VSAs represents the sunlight penetrating. This is then projected onto the plan. Similarly the parallel lines of HSAs in plan are drawn. Intersection of the projections of VSA lines from section, will give the area of sunlight penetration (ABCD) on the floor of the room. Areas of sunlight or shade do not have to be restricted to the floor. The sun may shine on the wall surfaces as well for low vertical and horizontal shadow angles. The basic principles described are applicable to any desired level above floor or ground level. The fraction of glass area under sunlight for a given louvre system can also be calculated by the formula

$$G = 1 - r_1 \tan(\text{VSA}) - r_2 \tan(\text{HSA}) + r_1 r_2 \tan(\text{VSA}) \tan(\text{HSA})$$

where G is the fraction of glass area sunlit, $r_1 =$ length of horizontal projection/window height, and $r_2 =$ length of vertical projection/window width.

3.10. SHADOW MASKS

In the earlier examples we have been concerned only with the shading at specified times only. However once a fixed type of louvre system is employed, the extent of shading and sunlight penetration will vary with the time of the day and the day of the year. To obtain a complete picture for the whole year a slightly different approach is required. The shadow angles may also be used to construct the outline of a projection for the wall or an external obstruction, 'as seen' from a given observation point. The outline of the obstructions is sometimes known as a 'shading mask' which when drawn on transparent material can be used as an overlay to a solar chart. From that the desired information, the sunlit and shaded periods for the whole year for the observation point can be directly noted.

In the construction of shading masks, the observation or reference point forms the centre of the diagram. The limits of the obstructions vertically and horizontally are plotted on a plan. The vertical limiting angles of obstructions determine the vertical shadow angles (VSAs); the horizontal limiting angles the horizontal shadow angles (HSAs). Thus the curved and radial lines on the shadow angle protractor can be used to plot the areas of obstructions. The shadow masks should be of the same radius (R) as that of the solar charts on which these are to be used as overlays. The construction of shadow masks for louvre systems fixed to building surfaces and external obstructions has been illustrated below with suitable examples.

Figure 3.13 is a shadow mask for an egg-crate louvre of 0·8-m width. First of all the vertical and horizontal angles the

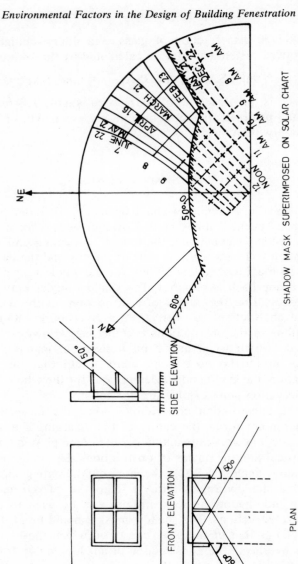

Fig. 3.13   Shadow mask for an egg-crate louvre.

louvre edges make at the middle point of the window are to be determined. These angles happen to be 50° and 60°, respectively, for this case. By placing a transparent paper on the shadow angle protractor and tracing the baseline, the semi-circular of 0° VSA, which represents the horizon, the central line marked which represents 0° HSA, and the curved line of 50° and two radial lines of 60° towards the right and left of the centre line. This forms the shade diagram for the louvre system under consideration for a reference point centrally located at the sill level of the window plane. All the periods covered by the

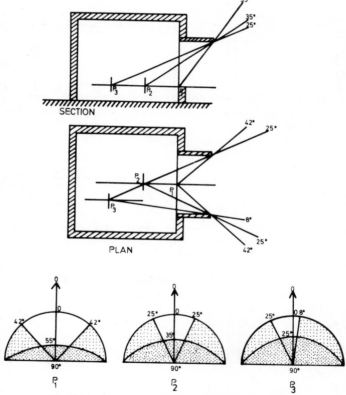

Fig. 3.14 Shadow masks for different points at sill level.

baseline and the limiting VSA and HSA shadow angle lines drawn, will be under shade and the rest of the time it will be exposed to the sunlight if the sun position at any time happens to be within this area of the diagram.

The shade mask thus prepared can then be placed over the solar chart with the central line coinciding the orientation of the building surface in question (north-east direction in this example). From this the days and times at which the window will be fully shaded can directly be noted.

Figure 3.14 illustrates more examples of shadow mask construction for reference points at different locations inside the

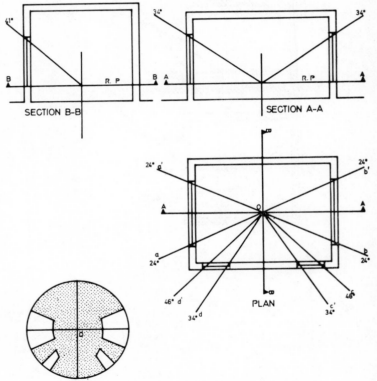

Fig. 3.15. Shadow mask for the centre of a room.

room. These diagrams provide a method of determining the extent of sunlight penetration into rooms with only one glazed wall.

Figure 3.15 illustrates the construction of shadow masks for the central point inside a room having walls with windows on three walls. It may be noted in such cases the outline of the shadow mask will be a full 360° diagram (a circle).

Figure 3.16 illustrates the construction of a shadow mask for

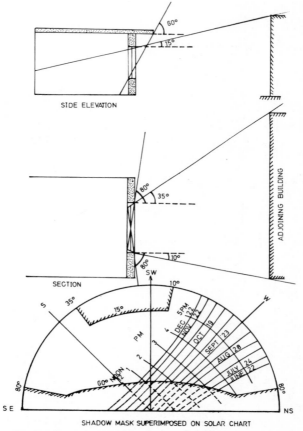

SHADOW MASK SUPERIMPOSED ON SOLAR CHART

Fig. 3.16. Shadow mask for a horizontal louvre and an external obstruction.

the combined effect of a horizontal projection to the wall over the window top and an external obstruction (a building). The vertical and horizontal limiting angles of the obstructing building for the window, can be found by drawing the lines from the building height to the top level of the window and from the edge of the horizontal projection to the sill level of the window (in

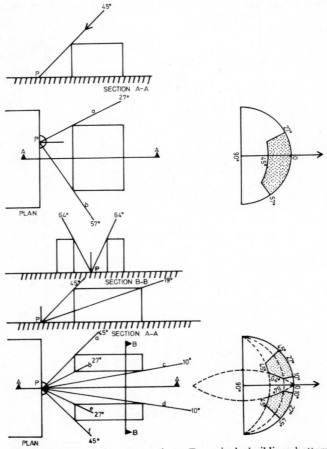

Fig. 3.17. Shadow mask for obstructions. Top, single building; bottom, two buildings.

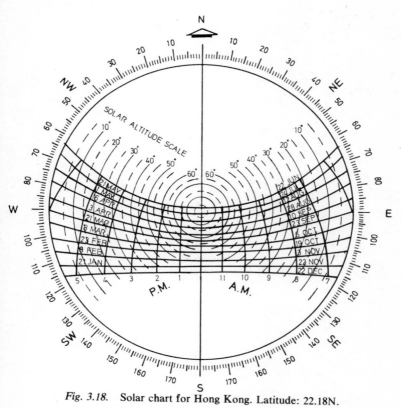

Fig. 3.18. Solar chart for Hong Kong. Latitude: 22.18N.

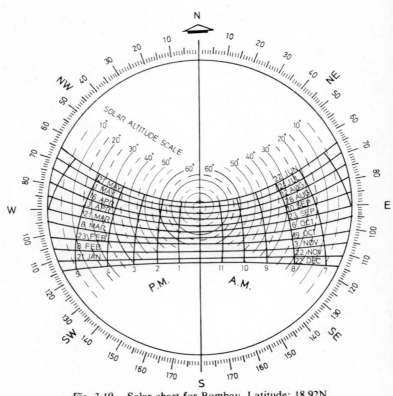

Fig. 3.19. Solar chart for Bombay. Latitude: 18.92N.

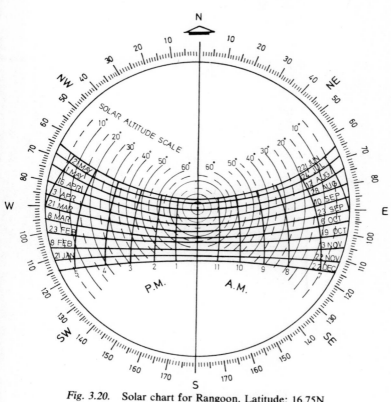

Fig. 3.20. Solar chart for Rangoon. Latitude: 16.75N.

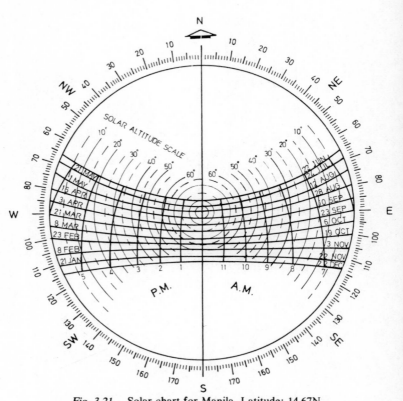

Fig. 3.21.   Solar chart for Manila. Latitude: 14.67N.

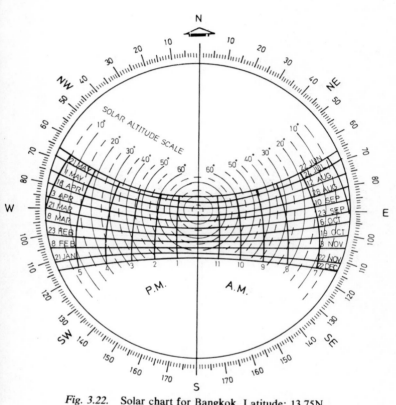

Fig. 3.22. Solar chart for Bangkok. Latitude: 13.75N.

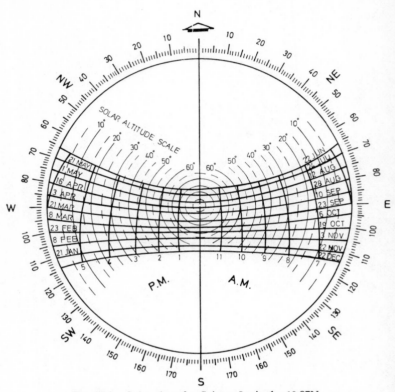

Fig. 3.23. Solar chart for Saigon. Latitude: 10.97N.

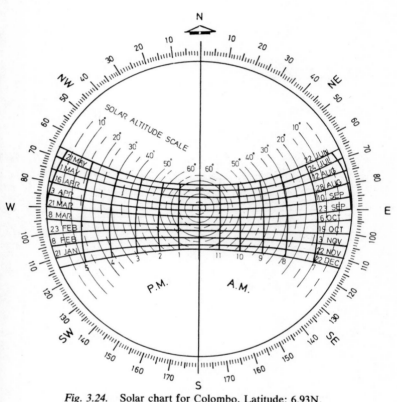

Fig. 3.24. Solar chart for Colombo. Latitude: 6.93N.

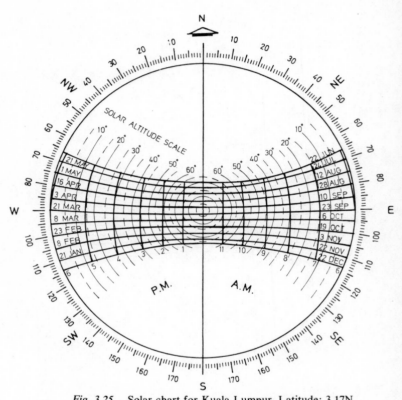

Fig. 3.25.   Solar chart for Kuala Lumpur. Latitude: 3.17N.

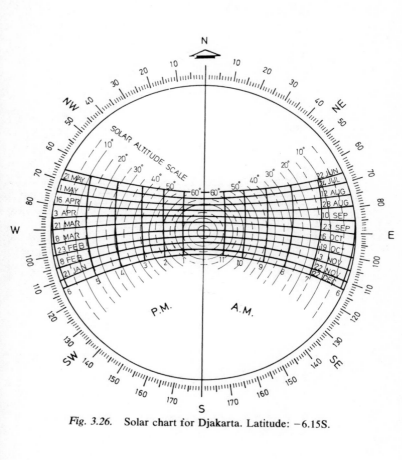

Fig. 3.26. Solar chart for Djakarta. Latitude: −6.15S.

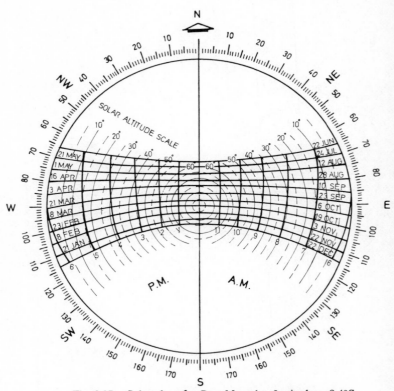

Fig. 3.27. Solar chart for Port Moresby. Latitude: −9.40S.

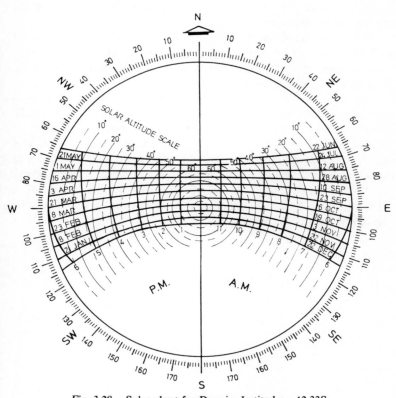

Fig. 3.28. Solar chart for Darwin. Latitude: −12.33S.

section) and from building corner points to the window edges in plan as shown in the figure. These angles are then measured (15° and 60° for VSA and 35° and 80° for HSA, respectively, for this example). The shading mask is then prepared for these limiting shadow angles by tracing these lines on the shadow angle protractor as explained earlier.

When this shadow mask is superimposed on the solar chart with the central line coinciding with the wall orientation (south-west in this case) on the solar chart, the periods of sunshine penetration can readily be noted.

Figure 3.17 illustrates two more examples on the construction of shadow masks for external obstructions for a single building and two buildings. Figures 3.18–3.28 show solar charts of 11 South-East Asian cities. It is important to note that the degree of obstruction given on the sun path overlay (shadow mask) is only applicable to the reference point. Other points on the building require the construction of a separate shading mask for each point. In practice it is usually only necessary to select critical points for analysis.

Chapter 4

Solar Radiation

Solar radiation as received on the surface of the earth is discussed in detail and methods of calculation are shown. Total, direct, and diffuse radiation are treated separately and the design and use of solar radiation protractors are illustrated.

4.1. INTRODUCTION

Solar radiation is an important factor in building design. Some of the basic decisions on orientation, glass area, type of glass and shading devices to be used are influenced by solar radiation. Architects and air-conditioning engineers require data on solar heat gains through various wall–window combinations for different orientations. Solar radiation at any place is highly variable as it depends on many factors which include astronomical, geographic, geometric and meteorological considerations.

In many countries, meteorological services make routine measurements of solar radiation on a horizontal surface. Meteorological services can rarely produce solar radiation data for all the localities where buildings are erected. Even for places for which they are available, the data are restricted to total (direct + diffuse) solar radiation on a horizontal surface. For building purposes solar insolation on vertical and inclined surfaces is also required. In general, no measured data for these surfaces are available.

It is usually recommended to use clear sky conditions for most design calculations and average day conditions which include the effect of clouds for energy-consumption estimates. For both the clear sky and average day conditions, direct and diffuse components are determined separately.

In the absence of measured data, computational methods

have been developed for the estimation of solar radiation intensities on any surface, and are used widely for solar heat-gain calculations of buildings.

All the estimation methods are based on the established measurements of (i) extraterrestrial solar radiation and its spectral energy distribution and (ii) the attenuation characteristics of atmospheric constituents as a function of wavelength.

This chapter will deal with the above two aspects and computational and graphical methods for the estimation of solar radiation intensities on building surfaces.

4.2. The Sun

The sun sustains life on the earth and is the ultimate source of most forms of energy available on the earth. It is also the chief influencing factor on the climate of different parts of the earth. Hence the sun has long been a subject of study and much valuable information has been accumulated. The basic data concerning the sun as a cosmic body are worth noting.

4.2.1. *Solar Distance*

The sun is a star around which the planet earth revolves in an elliptical orbit with the sun at one of the foci. The actual distance from the sun to the earth varies throughout the year. The shortest distance ($147 \cdot 1 \times 10^6$ km) occurs when the earth is in perihelion at about the 1st January while the longest distance ($152 \cdot 1 \times 10^6$ km) occurs when the earth is in aphelion at about the 1st July. The mean solar distance from the earth is taken as one-half of the perihelion and aphelion distances which is $149 \cdot 6 \times 10^6$ km. The radiation propagated from the sun takes about 8 min to reach the earth.

4.2.2. *Mass of the Sun*

The solar mass has been estimated to be about $2 \cdot 25 \times 10^{27}$ tons which is about 329 400 times greater than that of the earth. The diameter of the sun is 140 000 km which is over 100 times that of the earth. On the average, the solar disk subtends approximately 32 minutes of arc across its diameter. The mean solar density is calculated to be 1·4 times that of water.

4.2.3. *Energy of the Sun*

The total energy that the sun radiates into space is estimated to be $3·7 \times 10^{26}$ W of which the earth receives only a small fraction ($0·5 \times 10^{-9}$). Dividing the total energy radiated by the sun by its surface area we find that each square centimetre of the sun's surface radiates the energy of about 6000 W.

4.2.4. *Surface Temperature of the Sun*

Assuming that the sun radiates as a black body, from the Stefan–Boltzmann law the surface temperature of the sun is calculated as 5800°K. This is called the *effective temperature* of the sun.

4.2.5. *Brightness of the Sun*

It has been estimated that the total luminous flux of the sun is about 3×10^{27} candles. Dividing this by the solar surface area we find that the sun's surface brightness to be about 50 000 candles · cm^{-2}.

4.3. EXTRATERRESTRIAL SOLAR RADIATION

The extraterrestrial values of solar energy and its spectral distribution are of considerable importance for all solar energy applications on the earth's surface. These form the basis for computational methods of estimating solar radiation intensities at any place on the earth's surface. The subject of solar energy has been under active study for over half a century. Extensive measurements were made by several investigators at different locations and various altitudes. Based on these studies and some understanding of the atmospheric effects on solar radiant energy, extrapolations were made for solar radiation above the earth's atmosphere. This has led to the important finding that the solar radiation on a surface normal to the sun's rays, above the earth's atmosphere, does not vary with the altitude of the sun and is of a fairly constant value. This indirect inference has been confirmed in recent years by the direct measurements made by NASA through satellites equipped with more sophisticated equipment.

4.3.1. *Solar Constant* (I_{ON})

The solar constant has been defined as the energy received from the sun on unit area exposed normal to the sun's rays at the mean solar distance in the absence of earth's atmosphere. The actual numerical value for the solar constant has been revised constantly over the last several decades. The first figure provided by Abbot *et al.* [4.1] was $1.94 \, cal \cdot cm^{-2} \cdot mm^{-1}$ ($1353 \, W \cdot m^{-2}$). Later, this value was upgraded by the Smithsonian Institution to $1.97 \, cal \cdot cm^{-2} \cdot mm^{-1}$ ($1374 \, W \cdot m^{-2}$) and then to a value of $2.00 \, cal \cdot cm^{-2} \cdot min^{-1}$ ($1395 \, W \cdot m^{-2}$) based on Johnson's data [4.2]. However in the light of more recent data provided by Thekaekara [4.3] this value has been reverted

Table 4.1
Value of solar constant on the first day of each month

Date (1st of each month)	Value of solar constant ($W \cdot m^{-2}$)	Departure from mean percentage
January	1 399	+3·42
February	1 392	+2·96
March	1 378	+1·81
April	1 354	+0·16
May	1 331	−0·1·52
June	1 316	−2·79
July	1 309	−3·27
August	1 313	−2·84
September	1 328	−1·65
October	1 352	+0·03
November	1 375	+1·72
December	1 392	+2·96

to the original value of 1353 W · m^{-2}. The accuracy of the determination of this value is claimed to be within ±1·5%. According to definition, this value of the solar constant is applicable for the days of mean solar distance which occur only on the 4th April and the 5th October. The actual value for other days is subject to slight annual variations because of the variations in actual solar distance owing to the earth's orbital eccentricity. This maximum variation amounts to +3·42% around the 4th January and −3·27% around the 5th July. The values of solar constant on the first day of each month are given in Table 4.1.

Superimposed on the above annual cyclic variation there are very small additional variations caused by variations in solar weather and sun-spot activity cycles. However these can be neglected for terrestrial applications.

4.3.2. *Solar Spectral Energy Distribution*

The distribution of the energy received from the sun as a function of wavelength is also of considerable importance. The range of wavelengths of electromagnetic radiation spectrum emitted by the sun extends from a fraction of a millimicrometre ($<10^{-9}$ m) to hundreds of metres. However, the region between 0·28 μm to 3·0 μm caries about 98% of the total emitted energy. The solar spectral irradiance above the earth's atmosphere based on Thekaekara's data is shown in Fig. 4.1. This energy distribution in the sun's spectrum matches closely that of an ideal black body radiation at 5800°K. The greatest energy is radiated in the blue–green region of the spectrum for a wavelength of 0·48 μm. The intensity of radiation falls off from its maximum on either side, *i.e.* towards blue and red regions. However, the energy diminishes rapidly towards blue and more slowly towards the red. The percentage of the solar constant associated with wavelengths shorter than a given value are presented in Table 4.2. The best estimate would indicate broadly a spectral distribution of energy in the solar spectrum as 7–8% in the ultra-violet region, 41–42% in the visible region, and 51% in the infrared region.

Table 4.2

Percentage of solar constant associated with wavelengths shorter than λ (after Thekaekara [4.3])

Wavelength, λ (μm)	$P_{0-\lambda}$ (%)	Wavelength, λ (μm)	$P_{0-\lambda}$ (%)	Wavelength, λ (μm)	$P_{0-\lambda}$ (%)	Wavelength, λ (μm)	$P_{0-\lambda}$ (%)
0·22	0·050 2	0·52	25·379	0·85	59·899	6·0	99·719 5
0·23	0·097 1	0·53	26·742	0·90	63·365	7·0	99·823 3
0·24	0·143 0	0·54	28·084	0·95	66·556	8·0	99·881 5
0·25	0·194 4	0·55	29·38	1·0	69·488	9·0	99·916 7
0·26	0·269	0·56	30·648	1·1	74·435	10·0	99·939 2
0·27	0·405	0·57	31·907	1·2	78·404	15·0	99·981 7
0·28	0·564	0·58	33·176	1·3	81·652	20·0	99·992
0·29	0·810	0·59	34·439	1·4	84·331	25·0	99·996
0·30	1·210	0·60	35·683	1·5	86·639	50·0	99·999 5
0·31	1·655	0·61	36·902	1·6	88·611	100·0	99·999 0
0·32	2·218	0·62	38·098	1·7	90·261	200·0	99·999 99

0·33	2·928	0·63	39·270	1·8	91·593
0·34	3·721	0·64	40·421	1·9	92·644
0·35	4·517	0·65	41·550	2·0	93·489
0·36	5·316	0·66	42·657	2·1	94·202 4
0·37	6·150	0·67	43·744	2·2	94·826 9
0·38	7·003	0·68	44·810	2·3	95·373 9
0·39	7·819	0·69	45·855	2·4	95·858 0
0·40	8·725	0·70	46·879	2·5	96·290 3
0·41	9·920	0·71	47·882	2·6	96·671 0
0·42	11·222	0·72	48·864	2·7	97·007 3
0·43	12·473	0·73	49·826	2·8	97·310 3
0·44	13·725	0·74	50·769	2·9	97·583 8
0·45	15·140	0·75	51·691	3·0	97·827 7
0·46	16·653	0·76	52·595	3·5	98·620 0
0·47	18·167	0·77	53·480	4·0	99·057 9
0·48	19·681	0·78	54·346	4·5	99·337 4
0·49	21·155	0·79	55·194	5·0	99·512 2
0·50	22·599	0·80	56·023	400·0	99·999 99
0·51	24·015			1000·0	100·000 0

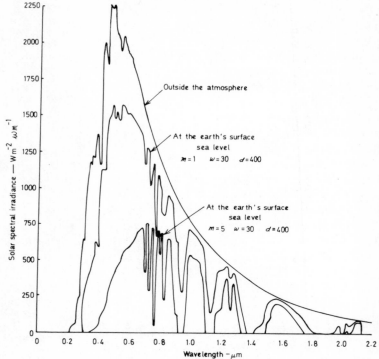

Fig. 4.1. Solar spectral energy distribution curves above the earth's atmosphere and at earth's surface (sea level) for air masses 1 and 5. (Adapted from *ASHRAE Trans.*, **64**, 50.)

4.4. ATMOSPHERIC EFFECTS

Our main interest lies in determining the intensity of solar radiation that actually reaches the earth's surface at any geographical location and its diurnal and annual variations.

The intensity and spectral energy distributions of solar radiation undergo significant modifications while passing through the layers of the earth's atmosphere. The extent to which the solar energy is depleted will depend upon the attenuation characteristics of the atmospheric constituents and the path length the sun's rays have to traverse through the atmosphere before reaching the earth's surface.

For many years scientists have studied the effects of the earth's atmosphere upon solar radiation. It has been established that for clear sky conditions the extinction due to atmosphere depends on two physical processes, namely scattering and absorption. The main constituents of the atmosphere such as air molecules, water-vapour molecules and dust particles, scatter the incoming radiation practically in all directions. Part of the radiation is absorbed mainly by ozone and oxygen in the upper atmosphere and by water vapour and carbon dioxide in the lower layers of the atmosphere. The scattering and absorption in the atmosphere vary along the path of the solar beam as the composition of the atmosphere is a function of height above the ground and also varies with time. The scattering and absorption coefficients of each atmospheric constituents further depend on the wavelength of the solar energy spectrum. Usually clear sky conditions do not prevail every day and as a rule clouds may intercept the sun at any moment and decrease the energy to a very low value. The type of the cloud and its coverage of the sky will determine the actual solar radiation reaching the ground surface during average days.

4.4.1. *Scattering*

The scattering effects differ for the air molecules, water-vapour molecules and the dust particles as they depend on the particle size with respect to the wavelength (λ). The well-known Rayleigh scattering theory is applicable only when the radius of the particle is less than $0\cdot1\ \lambda$ and for such cases the extinction is proportional to λ^{-4}. Scattering by dust-free air is the basic atmospheric effect. However scattering by dust particles often depletes much of the solar energy even at wavelengths greater than $1\ \mu$m. For particle sizes between the range of $0\cdot1\ \lambda$ and $25\ \lambda$ the more complicated Mei scattering theory is applied. In such cases the extinction is proportional to $\lambda^{-\alpha}$ and α frequently lies between 1 and 2. For fairly clear conditions α is generally taken as $1\cdot5$. For still larger size particles such as suspended water droplets the laws of geometrical optics may be applied to determine scattering effects.

In a dense layer of atmosphere the incident radiation may be scattered many times and some energy is scattered in the downward direction and a considerable proportion is also scattered in the upward direction. The intensity scattered in the backward direction is somewhat greater than the downward-scattered intensity. In Mei scattering, the amount of radiation in the forward direction is much larger than in the backward direction. In a mixture of particles exposed to the sun's rays, computations must involve integrals over the ranges of both wavelength and radius of the particles.

It is found that the total energy reflected back by a cloudless atmosphere is about 7%, which includes ozone absorption. The downward-scattered radiation is of diffuse nature and comes to the earth from the entire hemisphere dome of the sky.

4.4.2. *Absorption*

The main absorbing components of the atmosphere are oxygen, ozone, water vapour and carbon dioxide. Whereas atmospheric scattering is a continuous function of the wavelength, atmospheric absorption takes place in selected spectral bands.

Oxygen in the uppermost layers cuts off the extreme ultraviolet in the spectral range of $0 \cdot 12 – 0 \cdot 18 \, \mu$m.

Ozone absorbs in the spectral range of $0 \cdot 20$ and $0 \cdot 33 \, \mu$m and also to a small extent in the visible region of $0 \cdot 44$ and $0 \cdot 76 \, \mu$m. The ozone layer is located at altitudes between 10 and 50 km with a maximum concentration at 25 km. The total ozone content is estimated to be of the order of $1 \cdot 5$ and $4 \cdot 5$ mm at NTP. Owing to the oxygen and ozone absorptions, the energy in the spectral region, up to $0 \cdot 29 \, \mu$m does not, in practice, reach the earth's surface.

Water vapour has a number of absorption bands in the near infrared region, *viz*.: $0 \cdot 93$, $1 \cdot 13$, $1 \cdot 42$, $1 \cdot 47$, $1 \cdot 9$, $2 \cdot 7$, $3 \cdot 2$ and $6 \cdot 3 \, \mu$m.

Carbon dioxide also absorbs in the near infrared region at spectral bands of $1 \cdot 6$, $2 \cdot 0$, $2 \cdot 7$ and $4 \cdot 3 \, \mu$m. A significant percentage of the sun's radiation in the above spectral bands is cut off by these absorptions owing to water vapour and carbon dioxide.

Water vapour content decreases rapidly with height up to 4 km and becomes almost negligible above the tropopause. The total precipitable water content of the atmosphere will vary widely from place to place, with seasons, and from day to day at any given place.

4.4.3. *Air Mass*

Evidently the net attenuation of solar radiation intensity will also be a function of the path length the sun's rays have to traverse through the atmosphere to reach the earth's surface. The path length is usually expressed in terms of optical air mass (m). The air mass is a function of the solar zenith distance angle (z) and is approximately equal to sec z for zenith angles up to 70°. For zenith angles above 70° Bempoard's formula, which takes the earth's curvature and the refraction effects into account is generally applied. The air mass (m_0) at normal sea level pressure (P_0) as a function of solar altitude (θ) ($\theta = 90° - z$) is shown in Fig. 4.2.

For elevated places like hill stations, the mass of the atmosphere above will be less and hence it will be the reduced atmosphere that would prevail above that place. For such places, and for any other place with an atmospheric pressure (P) different from the normal sea-level pressure the corresponding air mass (m) can be obtained by

$$m \times P = m_0 \times P_0 \qquad (4.1)$$

where P_0 is the normal sea-level pressure (760 mmHg) and m_0 is the air mass at P_0.

4.4.4. *Solar Spectral Energy Distribution at Earth's Surface*

Moon [4.4] correlated the measured data obtained by Fowle, Abbot and others and arrived at an equation for total spectral transmissivity (T_λ) of the atmosphere due to scattering and absorption as a function of atmospheric pressure (p), precipitable water content (w), dust content (d), ozone content (O_3) and air mass (m) as

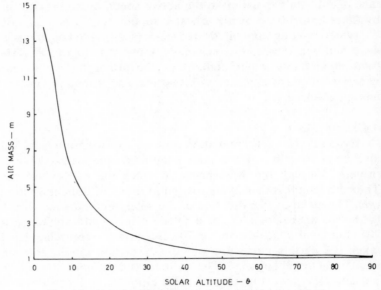

Fig. 4.2. Relationship between air mass and solar altitude.

$$T_\lambda = [(T_{am_\lambda})^{p/760}(T_{w_\lambda})^{w/20}(T_{d_\lambda})^{d/800}(T_{O_{3\lambda}})^{C_{O_3}/2\cdot5}(T^1_{w_\lambda})^{w/20}]^m \quad (4.2)$$

The first three terms refer to the effect of scattering by air molecules (am), water vapour (w) and dust particles (d) and the last two terms refer to the effect of absorption by ozone and water vapour respectively. T_λ is the monochromatic transmissivity for the wavelength (λ).

At any single wavelength, the monochromatic transmissivity may be calculated for various atmospheric conditions and air masses from the above eqn. (4.2). For each wavelength, by multiplying the spectral radiation intensity outside the earth's atmosphere ($I_{ON\lambda}$) with the corresponding monochromatic transmissivity of the atmosphere, the monochromatic direct radiation intensity ($I_{N,\lambda}$) at the earth's surface is obtained *i.e.*, $I_{N\lambda} = I_{ON\lambda}T_\lambda$.

Figure 4.1 shows typical results of calculated solar spectral energy distribution curves on clear days at sea level for air masses 1 and 5 for an assumed atmospheric condition of $w = 30$ mm; $d = 400$ particles/cm^3 and $O_3 = 2.5$ mm. This figure clearly illustrates the importance of the air mass (the path length of the sun's rays through the atmosphere) in reducing the solar radiation intensity.

4.4.5. *Atmospheric Transmission Factors* (*T*)

The overall atmospheric transmission factor (*T*) may be defined as the ratio between the integrated areas under the spectral energy distribution curves for a surface normal to the sun's rays at the earth's surface and above the earth's atmosphere. This may be expressed mathematically as

$$T = \frac{\int_0^\infty I_{ON\lambda} T_\lambda \, d\lambda}{\int_0^\infty I_{ON\lambda} \, d\lambda}$$

or

$$T = I_N / I_{ON} \tag{4.3}$$

Following the method of Moon [4.4] and Fritz [4.5*b*], Therlkeld and Jordan [4.6] computed the spectral solar radiation intensities, at sea level, for 63 chosen wavelengths between 0.295 and 2.13 μm for a wide range of atmospheric conditions. They had also determined the atmospheric transmission factors and presented in a graphical form as a function of air mass, precipitable water and dust contents for a fixed ozone value of 2.5 mm at NTP. These data in themselves are extremely valuable and make the problem of estimating direct solar radiation on clear days at the earth's surface relatively easy.

The transmission factors for direct solar radiation during clear days may vary from about 0.85 to less than 0.20 depending on the air mass and atmospheric conditions. It was found that for a given air mass and precipitable water content the transmission factor decreases linearly with the increasing dust content. At low values of precipitable water and large values of air mass, this decrease with the increase of dust content is greatest.

The effect of elevation upon the transmission factor has also been investigated. With other conditions constant, the total spectral transmissivity (T) increases as the barometric pressure decreases. Thus one would expect the transmission factor to increase for surfaces above sea level. The following empirical expression has been suggested [4.7] for the estimation of direct solar radiation for higher altitude stations

$$I_{N(h)} = I_{ON}T + I_{ON}a \times h(1 - T) \tag{4.4}$$

where $I_{N(h)}$ is the direct solar radiation on a surface normal to the sun's rays at a height h (km) above sea level, I_{ON} is the solar constant, a is an empirical constant the value of which is taken as $0\cdot14$/km, and T is the atmospheric transmission factor.

4.5. Solar Insolation Curves

Rao and Seshadri [4.8] have calculated the clear day direct solar radiation intensities on a surface normal to the sun's rays at sea level (I_N) as a function of solar altitude (θ) for a wide range of precipitable water and dust contents and have presented their results in a graphical form of a family of curves called solar insolation curves. Their original curves were based on Johnson's value of solar constant ($1395\ \text{W}\cdot\text{m}^{-2}$). As the most recently accepted figure for solar constant is $1353\ \text{W}\cdot\text{m}^{-2}$, a necessary correction factor must be applied to their data. The modified solar insolation curves are presented in Figs. 4.3–4.6. If these theoretical curves are to be used with greater confidence it is necessary to prove their reliability by comparison of the measured direct solar radiation under known atmospheric conditions with that obtained from the appropriate solar insolation curve. Rao and Seshadri [4.8] had also provided such a comparison for Roorkee. Spencer [4.9] provided a verification for Melbourne atmospheric conditions ($w = 10\ \text{mm}$ and $d = 300$ particles/cc). These comparisons are shown in Figs. 4.7 and 4.8 from which it can be clearly seen that the theoretical and measured data agree remarkably well in both the cases.

The precipitable water and dust content of the atmosphere vary considerably from place to place and time of the year for any given place. In tropical regions the precipitable water content will normally be low in the summer months and high in the monsoon periods. On the other hand, the dust content can be expected to be high in dry season and low in rainy months.

To some extent the variations in these two parameters exhibit self-compensatory effects. A very clear atmosphere may contain less than 200 dust particles/cc while an industrial atmosphere may contain as high as 800 aerosols/cc. Under equatorial climates high precipitable water content (40 mm or above) can be expected throughout the year.

The measured data on these atmospheric parameters are not readily available for many places. For many engineering applications estimates based on an assumed standard atmosphere, which may be arbitrarily defined, may be quite satisfactory. Wherever the observed data on the precipitable water and dust content are available or a reasonable guess can be made by choosing the appropriate solar insolation curve for each month, a better accuracy in the determination of direct solar radiation intensities can be expected.

For computer calculations it is desirable to express the solar insolation curves in an equation form in terms of solar altitude (θ). Spencer [4.10] has shown that each of the solar insolation curves can be expressed as a power series of $\sin \theta$ as

$$I_N = \sum_1^5 a_n \sin^n \theta$$
$$= a_1 \sin \theta + a_2 \sin^2 \theta + a_3 \sin^3 \theta + a_4 \sin^4 \theta + a_5 \sin^5 \theta \qquad (4.5)$$

The constants $a_1 a_2 \ldots \ldots a_5$ can be determined by the usual least squares method of curve fitting. The coefficients a_n were expressed as functions of precipitable water w (mm) in the form

$$a_n = B_{1n} + B_{2n} \log w + B_{3n} (\log w)^2 \qquad (4.6)$$

where B_{nm} are constants.

The coefficients of B_{nm} are given in matrix form as

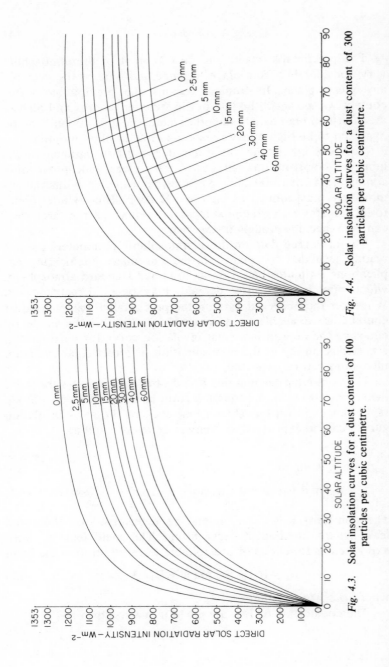

Fig. 4.3. Solar insolation curves for a dust content of 100 particles per cubic centimetre.

Fig. 4.4. Solar insolation curves for a dust content of 300 particles per cubic centimetre.

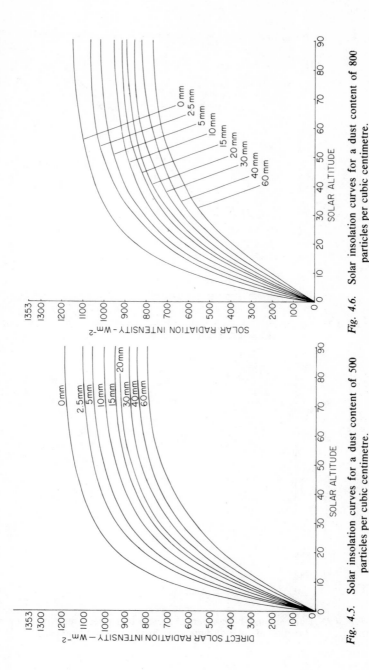

Fig. 4.5. Solar insolation curves for a dust content of 500 particles per cubic centimetre.

Fig. 4.6. Solar insolation curves for a dust content of 800 particles per cubic centimetre.

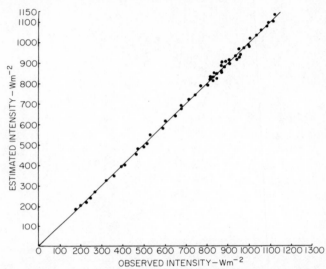

Fig. 4.7. Comparison of observed and estimated direct solar radiation intensities at Roorkee. (After Rao and Seshadri.).

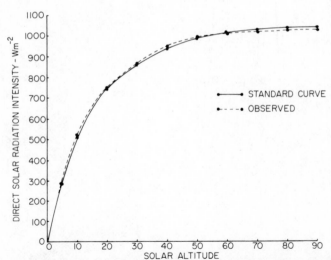

Fig. 4.8. Comparison of observed and estimated direct solar radiation as a function of solar altitude at Melbourne. (After Spencer.)

$$B = \begin{bmatrix} 9\cdot347\,110\,6 & -28\cdot526\,332\,9 & 48\cdot397\,587\,8 \\ -1\cdot042\,912\,9 & 5\cdot937\,930\,9 & -14\cdot213\,064\,1 \\ -0\cdot163\,097\,7 & 0\cdot207\,637\,3 & 0\cdot470\,318\,5 \end{bmatrix}$$

$$\begin{bmatrix} -41\cdot111\,749\,1 & 13\cdot349\,757\,2 \\ 15\cdot023\,700\,7 & -5\cdot759\,414\,5 \\ -1\cdot097\,638\,9 & 0\cdot566\,010\,7 \end{bmatrix}$$

The power series thus obtained for the direct solar radiation intensity in langleys $\cdot$ min^{-1} (g $\cdot$ cal $\cdot$ cm^{-2} $\cdot$ min^{-1}), on a surface normal to the solar beam (I_N). Over the range of precipitable water from 2–65 mm this expression represents the solar insolation curve family with an error rarely exceeding $\pm2\%$. This method has been employed by Spencer [4.11] in a computer program for the calculation of solar radiation tables for Australian state capital cities. As the values of I_N thus obtained are for mean solar distance correction factors given in Table 4.1 are to be applied for other times of the year.

4.5.1. *ASHRAE Method*

An alternative method given in the ASHRAE *Handbook of Fundamentals* [4.12] for the computation of direct solar radiation is widely used in USA. This method is also based on some assumed atmospheric conditions of ozone, precipitable water and dust content for each month. The monthly variation in the solar constant owing to changes in the solar distance from the earth is taken into account. The direct normal solar intensity is given by the expression

$$I_N = A/\exp(B/\sin\theta) \qquad (4.7)$$

where A is the extraterrestrial radiation on a normal surface and B is the atmospheric extinction coefficient for air mass of 1 (*i.e.* solar altitude 90°).

The values of A and B for the 21st of each month are given in Table 4.3. For locations where the atmospheric conditions differ considerably from those of the assumed conditions, the values of B given in Table 4.3 should be multiplied by the clearness factors appropriate for that place and month. Clearness factors for many American locations are provided by Therlkeld and Jordan [4.6].

It should be noted that the values of I_N obtained by these methods are representative of conditions on average cloudless days. The actual values on any particular day can be ±20% those for the average conditions depending upon the atmospheric clarity.

Table 4.3
Numerical values of the constants A, B and C

Date (21st of each month)	A (W · m⁻²)	B (air mass⁻¹)	C (dimensionless)
January	1 230	0·142	0·058
February	1 215	0·144	0·060
March	1 186	0·156	0·071
April	1 135	0·180	0·097
May	1 104	0·196	0·121
June	1 088	0·205	0·134
July	1 085	0·207	0·136
August	1 107	0·201	0·122
September	1 152	0·177	0·092
October	1 193	0·160	0·073
November	1 221	0·149	0·063
December	1 234	0·142	0·057

4.6. DIRECT SOLAR RADIATION ON ANY SURFACE

Solar radiation intensities on horizontal, vertical and sloping surfaces of any orientation are needed to assess solar heat gains of buildings. The irradiation on any surface at any latitude of the earth can be calculated if the radiation at the normal incidence (I_N) and the angle of incidence of the sun's rays with respect to the surface (i) are known. This is a relatively simple matter of the application of ray geometry. The solar angles with respect to a general case of inclined surface are defined in Fig. 4.9.

The direct solar radiation incident on any surface is obtained by multiplying the normal radiation (I_N) with the cosine of the angle of incidence (i) and is given as

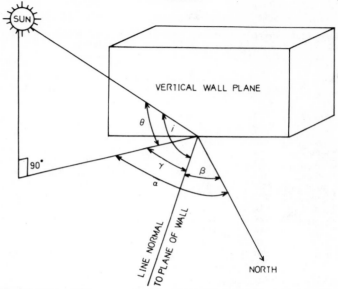

Fig. 4.9. Definition of solar angles with respect to a vertical surface. θ, solar altitude; α, solar azimuth; i, angle of incidence; β, wall azimuth; γ, wall solar azimuth.

$$I = I_N \cos i \qquad (4.8)$$

The angle of incidence for a sloped surface (i_s) can be expressed, in terms of solar angles (altitude θ and azimuth α) orientation angle (β) of the surface and the slope angle (φ), as

$$\cos i_s = \sin \theta \cdot \cos \varphi + \cos \theta \cdot \cos(\beta - \alpha) \cdot \sin \varphi$$

Horizontal and vertical surfaces are special cases of the above general surface, where $\varphi = 0°$ and $\varphi = 90°$, respectively. Thus for a horizontal surface, the angle of incidence (i_H) is given by

$$\cos i_H = \sin \theta \qquad (4.9)$$

and for a vertical surface

$$\cos i_V = \cos \theta \cdot \cos(\beta - \alpha) \qquad (4.10)$$

The expressions for the direct solar radiation for the horizontal, vertical and sloping surfaces will then be

Table 4.4
Hourly total (direct and diffuse) solar radiation on horizontal and vertical surfaces at Singapore (clear days)

Clock time	Horizontal	W · m⁻²							
		N	S	E	W	NE	SW	NW	SE
21st March									
7 a.m.	38	16	16	183	16	136	16	16	136
8 a.m.	246	60	60	593	60	435	60	60	435
9 a.m.	489	91	101	722	91	530	91	91	546
10 a.m.	707	120	132	681	120	508	120	120	527
11 a.m.	877	145	164	540	145	410	145	145	438
12 noon	981	161	183	334	161	268	161	161	296
1 p.m.	1 000	164	186	164	237	164	230	199	164
2 p.m.	931	151	174	151	457	151	382	353	151
3 p.m.	785	129	148	129	631	129	495	470	129
4 p.m.	584	104	114	104	726	104	552	533	104
5 p.m.	347	72	72	72	672	72	498	498	72
6 p.m.	110	35	35	35	391	35	287	287	35
22nd June									
7 a.m.	50	110	22	221	22	221	22	22	101
8 a.m.	243	271	60	527	60	543	60	60	243
9 a.m.	454	366	88	625	88	669	88	88	271
10 a.m.	644	423	114	584	114	669	114	114	224
11 a.m.	782	461	132	454	132	590	132	136	132
12 noon	864	476	145	271	145	470	145	290	145
1 p.m.	874	480	145	145	230	322	145	442	145
2 p.m.	808	464	136	136	423	167	136	568	136
3 p.m.	675	432	117	117	565	117	208	653	117
4 p.m.	495	385	95	95	628	95	268	678	95
5 p.m.	284	300	66	66	565	66	256	584	66
6 p.m.	85	148	28	28	300	28	136	303	28
22nd December									
7 a.m.	47	19	107	218	19	98	19	19	221
8 a.m.	249	60	293	552	60	243	60	60	577
9 a.m.	470	88	404	653	88	265	88	88	710
10 a.m.	666	113	473	606	113	208	113	133	713
11 a.m.	814	136	520	467	136	136	170	136	640
12 noon	896	145	536	268	145	145	337	145	508
1 p.m.	899	145	536	145	246	145	495	145	350
2 p.m.	823	136	520	136	451	136	628	136	183
3 p.m.	681	117	480	117	596	117	710	202	117
4 p.m.	492	91	413	91	653	91	716	262	91
5 p.m.	268	63	306	63	571	63	596	252	63
6 p.m.	63	25	129	25	265	25	268	120	25

$$I_{DH} = I_N \cdot \sin \theta \tag{4.11}$$

$$I_{DV} = I_N \cdot \cos \theta \cdot \cos(\beta - \alpha) \tag{4.12}$$

$$I_{DS} = I_N \cdot \sin \theta \cdot \cos \varphi + \cos \theta \cdot \cos(\beta - \alpha)\sin \varphi$$
or
$$I_{DS} = I_{DH} \cdot \cos \varphi + I_{DV} \cdot \sin \varphi \tag{4.13}$$

Using the above expressions and the methods of determining the normal radiation described earlier, calculated direct solar radiation data for different latitudes were presented in the ASHRAE *Handbook of Fundamentals* (*USA*) [4.12] and IHVE *Guide* (*UK*) [4.13]. Similar tables and graphs were also available for Australian cities [4.14] and Indian latitudes [4.15]. The reference data tables based on latitude can only be applicable for places on the same or near latitude by having similar atmospheric conditions assumed in the calculations of normal radiation (I_N). For more specific situations it is advisable to prepare reference solar data tables for each locality of interest, taking into account the average atmospheric conditions of that locality for each month. Further, it may also be more convenient to use solar radiation data produced on a clock time basis rather than for solar time, as people are more used to clock time in daily life.

For taking design decisions, clear day solar radiation data for three days in a year, equinox (21st March or 23rd September), summer solstice (22nd June) and winter solstice (22nd December), are sufficient. As an example hourly (clock time) direct solar radiations on clear days for the above three days for Singapore (1°28′N latitude) are presented in Table 4.4.

4.7. Diffuse Sky Radiation

While traversing through the atmosphere a part of the solar radiation becomes diffused by the process of scattering. The scattering functions involved are extremely complex and depend on the composition of the aerosols. The diffuse radiation comes from the whole upper hemisphere. The intensity of diffuse radiation from the sky vault on a horizontal surface may be of the order of 50–350 W · m^{-2} depending upon the atmospheric and cloud cover conditions. As a rule, on clear days it is usually small, comprising 10–15% of total (direct + diffuse) radiation, while on partially cloudy days it can form 30–45% of the total radiation received by a horizontal surface. The diffuse sky radiation contains mainly the visible and ultra-violet part of the sun's radiation, *i.e.* in the wavelength range of 0·29–1 μm. The zonal energy distribution in diffuse radiation spectrum depends on the solar altitude (θ), as can be seen from Table 4.5.

Table 4.5
Zonal energy distribution in diffuse radiation spectrum

Solar altitude, θ (°)	Percentage of the total sky radiation at:		
	<0·4 μm	0·4–0·6 μm	>0·6 μm
90	25·8	53·5	20·7
60	24·6	54·2	21·2
45	23·2	54·8	22·0
30	20·4	56·1	23·5
15	14·6	58·2	27·2
1	5·9	53·3	40·8

Diffuse radiation is more difficult to deal with as it is scattered through a wide range of angles and is not uniform in all directions. An important factor that contributes to the non-uniformity of diffuse sky radiation is the observed phenomenon of increased brightness of the patch of the sky in the region around the sun, called 'circum solar radiation'. Further, it has been observed that for clear skies the diffuse intensities are higher near the horizon than at the zenith. In the case of overcast skies it is the reverse, *i.e.* near the horizon it is darker than at the zenith.

4.7.1. *Diffuse Radiation on a Horizontal Surface* (I_{dh})

Measured data on diffuse radiation are scanty and are available for only a few locations. Based on the available data some empirical formulae have been proposed by Parmelea [4.16] and

Liu and Jordan [4.17] for the estimation of diffuse sky radiation from clear skies. Greater attention has been paid to this problem in recent years.

As in the case of direct radiation, diffuse radiation is also a function of solar altitude and increases with the increase of solar altitude. However increase in atmospheric turbidity increases diffuse radiation, while it reduces the direct as well as the net total solar radiation. Liu and Jordan [4.17] have obtained the following correlation between direct and diffuse transmissivities for a horizontal surface on clear days

$$T_d = 0 \cdot 2710 - 0 \cdot 2939 T_D \qquad (4.14)$$

where T_d is the transmission coefficient for diffuse solar radiation on a horizontal surface and is given by I_{dh}/I_{OH}; T_D is the transmission coefficient for direct solar radiation and is given by I_{DH}/I_{OH}; I_{OH} is the extraterrestrial radiation on a horizontal surface and is given by $I_{ON} \cdot \sin \theta$; and I_{DH} is the direct solar radiation on a horizontal surface at earth's surface and is given by $I_N \cdot \sin \theta$.

By substituting the expressions for T_d and T_D in the above equation we obtain an expression for diffuse radiation on a horizontal surface as

$$I_{dh} = (0 \cdot 2710 \, I_{ON} - 0 \cdot 2939 \, I_N) \sin \theta \qquad (4.15)$$

The constants obtained by Liu and Jordan may not be applicable for all places. They would depend on the atmospheric turbidity conditions of the place. For example, Spencer [4.9] obtained the values of $0 \cdot 3156$ and $0 \cdot 3288$ for the constants a and b for Melbourne. Hence a more general form of the equation for diffuse sky radiation would be

$$I_{dh} = (aI_{ON} - bI_N)\sin \theta \qquad (4.16)$$

Wherever possible the constants a and b are to be determined for local conditions in order to obtain reliable estimates of diffuse sky radiation.

The ASHRAE handbook [4.12] includes an approximate expression for diffuse sky radiation on a horizontal surface as

$$I_{dh} = C \cdot I_N \qquad (4.17)$$

where C is a dimensionless factor. The values of C for the 21st of each month are also given in Table 4.3 along with atmospheric extinction coefficient.

Ballantyne [4.18] has expressed the diffuse sky radiation on a horizontal surface as a power series of solar altitude; the equation for Melbourne is given as

$$I_{dh} = 438 \sin \theta - 1306 \sin^2 \theta + 2259 \sin^3 \theta - 1893 \sin^4 \theta$$
$$+ 618 \sin^5 \theta \ (W \cdot m^{-2})$$

A more general form would be

$$I_{dh} = C_1 \sin \theta + C_2 \sin^2 \theta + C_3 \sin^3 \theta + C_4 \sin^4 \theta + C_5 \sin^5 \theta$$
$$(4.18)$$

The constants $C_1, C_2 \ldots \ldots C_5$ are determined for each place based on measured data.

A simple method of estimating diffuse sky radiation from measured data of total radiation on a horizontal surface was developed by Penwarden [4.19] at the Building Research Station, UK. In this method the diffuse intensities on a horizontal surface are considered as the sum of two components: (i) 'background' diffuse component which is considered as uniform over the sky and (ii) a superimposed 'circum solar' component which can be treated geometrically as if it comes from the sun's beam radiation though in fact it comes from a region round the sun up to 30° wide. It has been observed that the background diffuse intensity depends only on the solar altitude and is independent of the clearness ratio. Mean values of background diffuse intensities on a horizontal surface for different solar altitudes for clear and partially cloudy skies are given in Table 4.6.

To obtain the 'augmented intensity' (direct + circum solar) the background diffuse radiation (I_{bH}) is subtracted from the total radiation intensity (I_{TH}) on a horizontal surface. The augmented direct intensities on a horizontal surface are then found from

$$I_{DH} = (I_{TH} - I_{bH}) \qquad (4.19)$$

Table 4.6
Background diffuse intensities I_{bH} on horizontal

Solar altitude, θ (°)	Background diffuse intensity (W · m⁻²)	
	cloudless skies	partially clouded skies
10	41	50
20	63	101
30	76	151
40	85	202
50	95	252
60	101	303

The direct solar radiation intensities on any surface are then obtained from

$$I_{DS} = (I_{TH} - I_{bh}) \cdot \cos i_s / \cos i_H \qquad (4.20)$$

4.7.2. *Diffuse Radiation on Vertical Surfaces*

Diffuse short-wave radiation on vertical surfaces is made up of two parts, namely, radiation diffusely scattered from the sky and radiation diffusely reflected from the ground and surrounding building surfaces. Parmelea [4.16] has made a series of measurements on diffuse radiation on a vertical surface under cloudless sky conditions and presents a series of curves. An equation of the form given below fits this family of curves reasonably well.

$$I_{dV} = K_1 \sin \theta + K_2 \sin^2 \theta \cdot \cos \theta \cdot \cos if(i) \qquad (4.21)$$

The first term of this equation is intended to represent the radiation from the sky vault and the reflected radiation from the ground. The second term will represent radiation from the part of the sky immediately around the sun (circum solar radiation).

and
$$f(i) = 1 \text{ for } 0 \leq i \leq 90°$$
$$f(i) = 0 \text{ for } i > 90° \qquad (4.22)$$

The values of constants K_1 and K_2 depend on the atmospheric turbidity of the place. Typical values of K_1 and K_2 found by Parmelea are 167 W $\cdot$ m^{-2} and 85 W $\cdot$ m^{-2}. Spencer's studies gave the values of 208 W $\cdot$ m^{-2} and 69 W $\cdot$ m^{-2} for K_1 and K_2, respectively, at Melbourne.

The ASHRAE handbook adopted Therlkelds findings on the diffuse radiation on a vertical surface (on clear days). It is given as a function of I_{dh} and the cosine of the incidence angle for the surface as

$$I_{dV} = I_{dh}[0\cdot55 + 0\cdot437 \cos i_v + 0\cdot313 \cos^2 i_v] \qquad (4.23)$$

for cases where $\cos i > -0\cdot2$, and otherwise $I_{dV} = 0\cdot45 I_{dh}$. Wherever the total radiation and diffuse radiation on a horizontal surface are available, the diffuse sky radiation on a vertical surface can be calculated from the expression

$$I_{dV(sky)} = (I_{TV} - I_N \cdot \cos i_v) \qquad (4.24)$$

where $I_N = (I_{TH} - I_{dh})/\sin \theta$. The ground-reflected component can be separately obtained by the formula

$$R_{gv} = \tfrac{1}{2} \rho I_{TH} \qquad (4.25)$$

where R_{gv} is the ground-reflected diffuse radiation on a vertical surface, ρ is the reflection factor for the ground, and I_{TH} is the total (direct + diffuse) solar radiation on a horizontal surface.

The albedo of the ground surface should be determined locally, in view of the wide variations which occur with different types of ground, covered or not with vegetation which will vary according to season and rainfall. It would appear reasonable to adopt values of the order of $0\cdot20$–$0\cdot25$ on sites of green vegetation, and $0\cdot1$–$0\cdot15$ on central urban sites where buildings and road surfaces predominate. An important factor influencing the radiation balance of vertical and inclined surfaces is the change of albedo of the ground surface with the angle of incidence. The albedo increases very appreciably at low angles of incidence. Another important factor is that appreciably higher diffuse radiation is received from the quadrant of the sky facing the sun than from the quadrant of the sky facing away from the sun.

The total diffuse radiation on a vertical surface will then be

$$I_{dV} = I_{dV(sky)} + R_{gv} \qquad (4.26)$$

4.7.3. *Diffuse Radiation on Inclined Surfaces*

Much less is known about diffuse radiation on sloping surfaces than on vertical surfaces. Measured data are scanty. Because of the relatively low intensity of the diffuse radiation, the approximation based on the $\cos^2 \varphi/2$ law may in general be sufficient for estimating diffuse sky radiation on a tilted surface, *i.e.*

$$I_{dS(sky)} = I_{dh} \times \cos^2 \varphi/2 \qquad (4.27)$$

where φ is the slope angle of the tilted surface with respect to horizontal.

The ground-reflection component on the tilted plane can be fairly estimated by the expression

$$R_{gs} = \rho \times I_{TH} \times \sin^2 \varphi/2 \qquad (4.28)$$

Thus the total diffuse radiation (sky + ground reflection) on a sloped surface will be

$$I_{ds} = I_{dh} \cdot \cos^2 \varphi/2 + \rho I_{TH} \cdot \sin^2 \varphi/2 \qquad (4.29)$$

As mentioned earlier, the diffuse sky radiation distribution in the sky vault is not isotropic on cloudless days. The isotropic assumption overestimates the diffuse radiation on surfaces away from the sun approximately by about 20–25% and underestimates by a similar percentage range on surfaces in the quadrant of the sun. On overcast conditions, the diffuse radiation on vertical and tilted surfaces can be estimated satisfactorily by the isotropic assumption. There appears to be no published information about the anisotropy of the diffuse radiation on partly cloudy conditions, but qualitative observations show that there are two main factors influencing the diffuse radiation distribution, namely: (i) a tendency to find regions of high brightness on clouds which stand opposite the sun, giving significant back reflection; and (ii) a tendency to find regions of high brightness of cloud close to the sun.

4.7.4. *Total Radiation Intensities on Vertical and Sloping Surfaces*

The total radiation intensity on any surface is the sum of direct radiation from the sun, diffuse sky radiation and the diffuse reflected radiation from the ground and surrounding surfaces. These can be expressed in terms of total radiation and background diffuse radiation on a horizontal surface as

(i)   *Vertical surfaces*

$$I_{TV} = (I_{TH} - I_{bH}) \frac{\cos i_v}{\cos i_H} + \tfrac{1}{2} I_{bH} + \tfrac{1}{2} \rho_g I_{TH} \qquad (4.30)$$

(ii)   *Sloping surfaces*

$$I_{TS} = (I_{TH} - I_{bH}) \frac{\cos i_s}{\cos i_H} + \cos^2 \varphi/2 I_{bH} + \sin^2 \varphi/2 \times \rho_g I_{TH}$$

$$(4.31)$$

Loudon's [4.20] work indicates that the above mathematical models which were first proved accurate for cloudless sky are also found to fit well for partially clouded skies.

4.7.5. *Solar Radiation on Average Days*

So far we have considered solar radiation on clear days. The effects of clouds have not been taken into account. Clouds are complex phenomena varying from thin transparent cirrus clouds exerting little influence on total (global) radiation to thick dark cumulus clouds which diminish the total radiation considerably. The brightness of cumulus clouds may greatly vary depending on their position with regard to sun. It is obvious that the actual radiation received at the earth's surface will largely depend on the cloud amount, the type of clouds and their distribution in the sky prevailing at a given time and location. The influence of clouds on the radiation balance is accounted for statistically. However individual cases may depart considerably from average conditions. Separate values of direct and diffuse components should be examined.

It is a common observation that the decrease of the direct component owing to cloud cover is accompanied by increased diffuse radiation though the total radiation itself is reduced.

Partially cloudy conditions result in many types of radiation records. The size, and speed of translation and number of clouds determine the duration and frequency of transients in direct

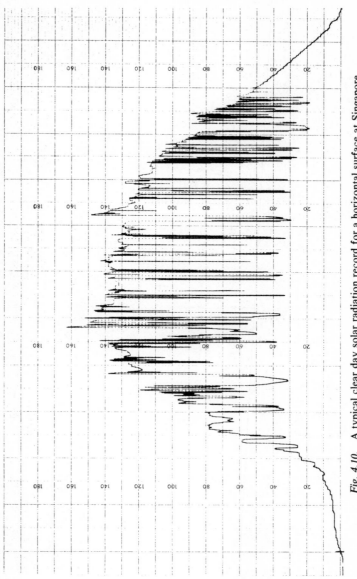

Fig. 4.10. A typical clear day solar radiation record for a horizontal surface at Singapore.

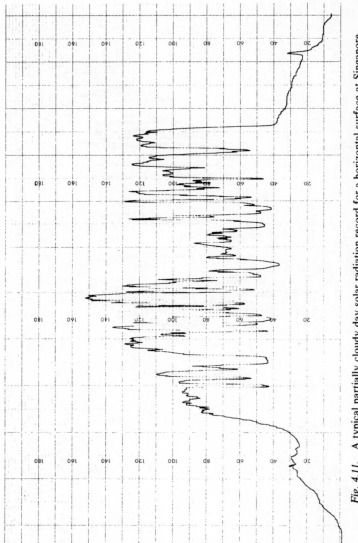

Fig. 4.11. A typical partially cloudy day solar radiation record for a horizontal surface at Singapore.

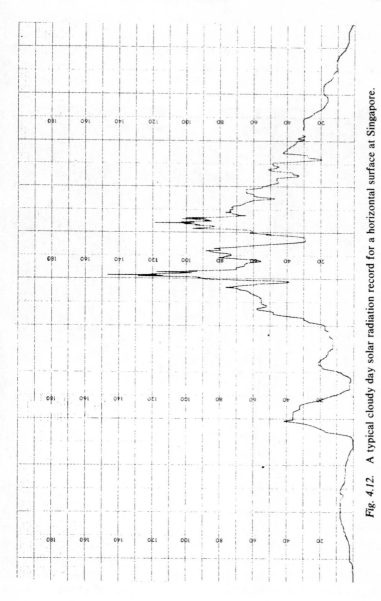

Fig. 4.12. A typical cloudy day solar radiation record for a horizontal surface at Singapore.

beam irradiance. The amplitudes of these fluctuations primarily depend upon the extent to which the clouds transmit the direct beam. These are illustrated in Figs. 4.10–4.12 for clear, partially cloudy and cloudy days, respectively. The measuring devices are shown in Figs. 4.13–4.15. The total radiation on a horizontal

Fig. 4.13.   Kipp and Zonen solarimeter with shade ring for the measurement of diffuse radiation.

surface can be considered as a sum of three components, *viz.* direct radiation from the sun, diffuse radiation from the blue part of the sky and diffuse radiation from the clouds.

$$I_{\text{TH}} = I_D(1 - C) + I_{\text{dh(blue sky)}} + I_{\text{dh(cloud)}} \qquad (4.32)$$

where C is the cloudiness.

However, in spite of these difficulties some attempts were made by several investigators [4.21, 4.22] to establish empirical relations in a general way to estimate the global radiation on average days which take the influence of clouds into account. In these attempts the duration of actual bright sunshine hours is

Fig. 4.14. Kipp and Zonen and Eppley black and white pyranometer for measurement of diffuse and total radiation respectively.

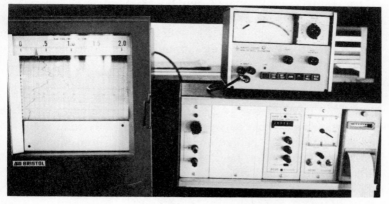

Fig. 4.15. Strip-chart potentiometric millivolt recorder, lintronic dual-channel electronic integrator with Sedco printout system.

taken as a measure of cloudiness. The general expression for total solar radiation received by a horizontal surface is given as

$$Q = Q_0(a + bS_a/S_b) \qquad (4.33)$$

where Q is mean daily total radiation on a unit area of a horizontal plane for the period under consideration (usually one month); Q_0 is the daily total radiation on a horizontal plane above the earth's atmosphere for the same period under consideration; 'a' and 'b' are constants depending on locality and atmospheric conditions such as water vapour, dust, type of clouds, *etc.* at that place; S_a is the mean daily amount of bright sunshine hours during the period under consideration; and S_b is the possible sunshine hours per day during the period under consideration.

In the absence of local records considerable meteorological intelligence must be used while selecting the values of 'a' and 'b' for a particular place or region. The mean values of 'a' and 'b' are found to be 0·29 and 0·52, respectively. It should be remembered that these formulae give only an approximate estimation of mean daily total radiation received for typical average days. The average amount of radiation intensities on vertical and inclined surfaces can be calculated only if the diffuse radiation component can be assessed with reasonable accuracy. These relations are useful to estimate the mean daily total and diffuse radiations for average days for places where not even the total radiation measurements are available and only sunshine hours data are obtainable.

4.7.6. *Diffuse Radiation on Average Days*

Several investigators [4.23, 4.24] have attempted to establish empirical relationships between the average daily total radiation Q and daily diffuse radiation D_H. The regression equation for diffuse radiation has been found to be non-linear and of parabolic form and is given as

$$D_H = (c \cdot Q + dQ^2/Q_0)$$

or

$$D_H/Q = (c + dQ/Q_0) \tag{4.34}$$

where 'c' and 'd' are constants which are determined by a regression analysis of the measured data. Mean values of 'c' and 'd' are found to be 1·00 and 1·13, respectively.

The ratio of D_H/Q reaches 1·00 on overcast days. Low values of D_H/Q are normally associated with regions of great atmospheric clarity (less turbid) and high values with regions of high turbidity. The maximum value of D_H occurs on partially cloudy days, when S_a/S_b is between 0·4 and 0·5, but not on clear or overcast days. Calculations for humid tropical regions show that nearly one-half of the mean daily total radiation on a horizontal surface is diffuse scattered radiation. All the observations confirm the fact that linear interpolation between diffuse radiation on clear days and overcast days gives completely erroneous results. The theoretical parabolic relationship provides estimates of daily total diffuse radiation with reasonable accuracy.

The effect of cloudiness on radiation falling on vertical and tilted planes is very dependent on the position of the sun. The radiation from clouds is much more sensitive to the albedo of the underlying ground than the radiation from the ground. Much depends on the characteristics of the clouds. In any case, the problem of clouds can only be solved by statistical methods based on long-term measurements and individual cases may depart considerably from the average conditions. Liu and Jordan [4.17] have obtained empirical correlations between monthly average daily diffuse radiation ($\bar{D}$) and monthly average daily total radiation ($\bar{Q}$) on a horizontal surface for average days, as a function of average cloudiness index ($\bar{K}_T$), *i.e.* ($\bar{Q}/\bar{Q}_0$). This correlation is expressed as

$$\bar{D}/\bar{Q} = 1\cdot390 - 4\cdot027(\bar{K}_T) + 5\cdot531(\bar{K}_T)^2 - 3\cdot108(\bar{K}_T)^3 \quad (4.35)$$

4.7.7. *Hourly Diffuse Radiation on Average Days*

Liu and Jordan [4.17] have also found a relationship between average hourly diffuse ($\bar{I}_{dh}$) and average daily diffuse radiation ($\bar{D}$), and average hourly total ($\bar{I}_{TH}$) and average daily total ($\bar{Q}$) radiation on a horizontal surface. A set of curves of R_d, *i.e.* ($\bar{I}_{dh}/\bar{D}$) and R_T, *i.e.* ($\bar{I}_{TH}/\bar{Q}$) as a function of possible sunshine hours is produced. For equatorial regions where the maximum possible sunshine hours are 12 h throughout the year, the values obtained for R_d and R_T at different hours of the day are given in Table 4.7.

From the above relations the hourly diffuse and total radiation values can be determined if the daily diffuse and daily total

Table 4.7
Values of R_d and R_T

Solar time	$R_d(\bar{I}_{dh}/\bar{D})$	$R_T(\bar{I}_{TH}/\bar{Q})$
6–7 17–18	0·018	0·013
7–8 16–17	0·052	0·044
8–9 15–16	0·080	0·079
9–10 14–15	0·094	0·107
10–11 13–14	0·104	0·124
11–12 12–13	0·109	0·132

radiation values are available for average days in each month. Garg [4.25] has found that estimates obtained by these expressions agreed reasonably well with the measured values at Roorkee, India. The estimates obtained by these empirical correlations are expected to be within ±5%.

Recently Orgill and Hollands [4.26] have arrived at simple correlation equations for hourly diffuse radiation on a horizontal surface in terms of k_d, *i.e.* (I_{dh}/I_{TH}) and k_T, *i.e.* (I_{TH}/I_{OH}) for overcast, partially cloudy and clear sky conditions as

Overcast skies i.e., $k_T < 0·35$

$$k_d = 1·0 - 0·249\,k_T \qquad (4.36)$$

Partially cloudy conditions i.e., $0·35 > k_T < 0·75$

$$k_d = 1·557 - 1·84\,k_T \qquad (4.37)$$

and

Clear sky conditions i.e., $k_T > 0·75$

$$k_d = 0·177 \qquad (4.38)$$

From the above empirical expressions, the hourly diffuse radiation values can be estimated approximately if the measured values of hourly total (direct + diffuse) radiation is available.

However for better accuracies such correlations are determined for each place or region as the type and amount of clouds vary over a wide range from place to place and from month to month.

4.8. Solar Radiation Protractors

The computational methods elaborated in the previous section would prove very laborious to compute radiation intensities on building suffaces hour by hour. Though with the aid of digital computers a large number of reference data tables for different latitudes and orientations can be prepared at length, they may not be the most convenient form of presentation for the use by architects and designers.

An alternative approach which is more attractive to architects for obtaining the required information on solar heat gains of walls and roofs in a quick way is to use a set of protractors made of transparent material (overlays) in conjunction with the sun path diagram (solar chart) of the latitude concerned. The construction and use of solar charts and shadow angle protractors is explained in Chapter 3. Here we will confine ourselves to the construction and use of solar radiation protractors.

4.8.1. *Design of Direct Radiation Protractors*

The basis for the design of a direct radiation protractor is the same as that for the computational method, namely the 'solar insolation curve' for the assumed standard atmospheric conditions, *i.e.* 760 mm of atmospheric pressure, 2·5 mm of ozone, 15 mm of precipitable water and 300 dust particles/cc. The intensity of solar radiation on a surface normal to sun's rays (I_N) is a function of solar altitude (θ). The intensity of solar radiation on a horizontal surface at a given time is given as $I_{DH} = I_N \cdot \sin \theta$ and on a vertical surface it also depends on the solar azimuth (α) and wall orientation angles (β).

$$I_{DV} = I_N \cos \theta \cdot \cos(\beta - \alpha) \qquad (4.39)$$

where $(\beta - \alpha)$ is also called wall solar azimuth angle. The maximum value of direct solar radiation on a horizontal surface will be obtained when the solar altitude is 90° and is equal to 990 W · m^{-2} for the standard conditions.

Using the above equations, the values of direct solar radiation received by a surface at various solar altitudes and wall solar azimuth angles can be tabulated. The solar radiation intensities can either be directly used or can be expressed as a ratio of the maximum value of radiation, *i.e.* I_N at solar altitude of 90°. Using the tabulated data, contours of equal solar radiation or radiation ratios can be constructed.

4.8.1.1. *Horizontal surface protractor*

For a horizontal surface, these equiradiation contours will form concentric circles. A series of such concentric circles can thus be drawn over a stereographic projection of the sky vault to the same scale of the solar chart. These provide solar radiation or radiation ratios for corresponding solar altitudes. Such a protractor which is made of a transparent material, when placed directly over a solar chart, the radiation values or ratios, can be read directly for the required time and day. In the case of a radiation ratio protractor, the solar radiation value is obtained by the product of the ratio and the possible maximum radiation value is 990 W · m^{-2}.

4.8.1.2. *Vertical surface protractor*

Contours of equiradiation or radiation ratios can be constructed for vertical surfaces. A contour line linking the various angles of azimuth will indicate the position of the sun where a certain radiation value can be obtained. The radiation protractor may be placed on a solar chart and be turned to the required orientation of the wall concerned. Then the values of radiation or ratios can be read directly for the required time and day. As in the above, in the case of ratio protractor, the solar radiation value is obtained by the product of the ratio and the maximum possible radiation value ($I_{N(max)}$) *i.e.* 990 W · m^{-2}.

An equiradiation ratio protractor for horizontal and vertical surfaces, which are combined in one diagram, is shown in Fig. 4.16. The contours are given in steps of ratios of 0·1. One half

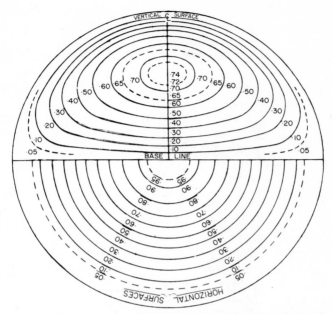

Fig. 4.16. Solar radiation protractor for horizontal and vertical surfaces.

(semi-circle) provides radiation ratio concentric circles for horizontal surfaces and the other half provides equiradiation ratio contours for vertical surfaces. The baseline represents the vertical surface and the central line designates the surface orientation. It can be seen that on a vertical surface the highest ratio of 0·74 will be obtained. This would occur when the solar altitude of 30°.

Use of these radiation protractors is illustrated through examples in Figs. 4.17 and 4.18.

(i) *To find the solar radiation received on a horizontal sur-*
face (flat roof) at 10 a.m. (solar time) on the 22nd June at
Singapore. Superimpose the half of the radiation ratio protractor relating the horizontal surface over the solar chart for Singapore latitude as illustrated in Fig. 4.17. The intersection at 10 a.m. hour line and the 22nd June sun path line gives the radiation

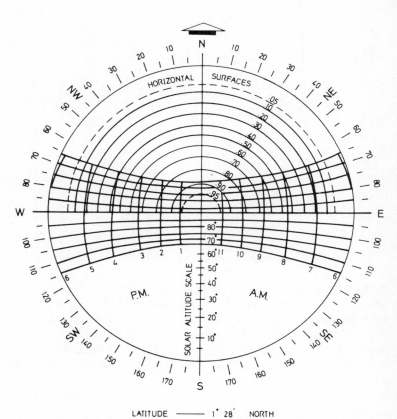

LATITUDE ———— 1° 28' NORTH

Fig. 4.17. Illustration of the use of solar radiation protractor in conjunction with a solar chart, for a horizontal surface.

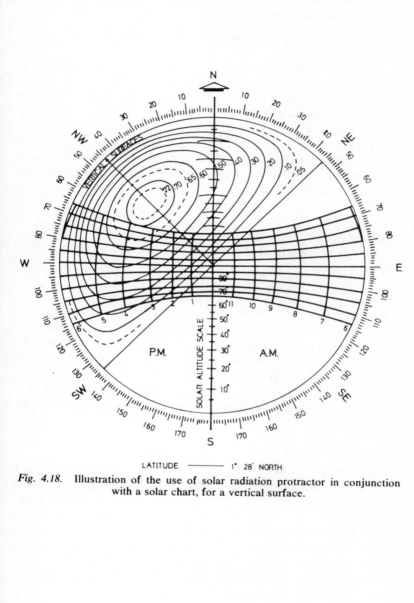

Fig. 4.18. Illustration of the use of solar radiation protractor in conjunction with a vertical surface.

ratio of 0·75 (by intrapolation). The direct solar radiation on a horizontal surface would then be

$$I_{DH} = 0.75 \times 990 = 732.5 \text{ W} \cdot \text{m}^{-2}$$

(ii) *To find the solar radiation received by a vertical wall of north-west orientation at 4 p.m. (solar time) on the 22nd June.* Superimpose the half of the radiation ratio protractor for vertical surfaces on the solar chart for Singapore with the centre line of the protractor pointing at the N-W direction on the solar chart, as illustrated in Fig. 4.18. The radiation ratio at the point of intersection of the hour line and the 22nd June sun path line is found to be 0·69 (by intrapolation). The direct solar radiation intensities on the north-west wall would then be

$$I_{DV(NW)} = 0.69 \times 990 = 683.1 \text{ W} \cdot \text{m}^{-2}$$

Radiation protractors for inclined surfaces, (one for each slope angle) can be constructed following the above procedures using the expression

$$I_{DS} = I_N(\sin \theta \cdot \cos \varphi + \cos \theta \cdot \cos(\beta - \alpha)\sin \varphi)$$

where φ is the slope angle with respect to the horizontal.

Diffuse radiation protractors for clear days, for horizontal and vertical surfaces are also available [4.27] based on the empirical correlations obtained between solar altitude and diffuse radiation intensities, by Parmelea [4.16] for standard atmospheric conditions. A more comprehensive series of radiation overlays (protractors) is provided by the Building Research Station, UK [4.28].

4.8.2. Correction Factors for Dust Content

As in the case of computational methods, suitable correction factors are applied to the radiation data obtained by the solar radiation protractors for atmospheric conditions which differ considerably from those of assumed standard conditions. For a more accurate estimate, the protractors should be constructed based on the appropriate solar insolation curve. On the other hand, suitable correction factors are to be applied to the values obtainable by the protractors designed for standard conditions.

Table 4.8
Correction factors for dust contents [a]

Solar altitude, θ (°)	Correction factor at:			
	100/cc	300/cc	500/cc	800/cc
10	1·16	1·00	0·88	0·73
20	1·08	1·00	0·94	0·83
30	1·05	1·00	0·95	0·89
40	1·04	1·00	0·96	0·89
50	1·03	1·00	0·96	0·90
60	1·03	1·00	0·96	0·90
70	1·03	1·00	0·97	0·91
80	1·03	1·00	0·97	0·92
90	1·03	1·00	0·97	0·92

[a] Dust content in particles/cc.

Correction factors for dust contents other than 300 dust particles/cc are given in Table 4.8. It can be seen that the correction factors are also a function of solar altitude. To obtain the direct solar radiation for dust contents other than 300 particles/cc, the values obtained by the protractor are multiplied by the corresponding correction factor.

It is obvious that the accuracy obtained by these protractors is rather limited as some intrapolation is required for intermediate values of radiation ratios. However the ease of operation and quick estimation of the solar radiation on any surface are the major advantages of this method.

As a very high accuracy is not really required for building design purposes, the radiation protractors have in fact proved popular with architects and designers.

Chapter 5

Effect of Wind on Window Design

The effect of wind on buildings, including the design wind speed and wind load, air flow around buildings, and wind load on wall claddings is discussed. The mechanical properties of ordinary glass with reference to its fatigue strength are shown. Some tests on glass are listed. Design of window glazing and strength of window frames and assembly are briefly mentioned.

5.1. INTRODUCTION

The effect of wind on windows, especially against glazing, has not been a problem in building design until the advent of large window areas. They have been made popular in modern building design following the development of 'picture windows' when uninterrupted view is available by the use of plate glass and strong framing. Large glass panels are synonymous with prestige and prosperity.

The problem with wind load against buildings, hitherto not considered in the design of windows, has now become important. As the glass sheet is basically a thin plate structure it requires strong support around its edges, and the central point is not to deflect beyond its limit of elasticity, otherwise cracking and shattering of the glass sheet may occur. Similarly the mullions and transoms which are used to support the glass sheets are also required to be of sufficient strength so as to minimise the deflection and bending.

The behaviour of glass sheets under wind load, the maximum allowable deflection, and the method of glazing are therefore important factors to be considered in the design of windows.

5.2. WIND AND BUILDING

Wind is generated when the earth's atmosphere is differentially heated by solar radiation. Changes in the air temperature in the atmosphere in turn change the density and pressure of the air, thus causing air movement from regions of high pressure to regions of low pressure. In addition, the rotation of the earth, too, causes air movement which becomes steadier at a height of about 400 m under normal conditions. In an open channel flow, the mean velocity decreases to zero towards the surface owing to shear drag. Similarly, the air flow over the earth's surface is reduced to zero at the ground level owing to the frictional drag, and obstructions to airflow caused by man-made structures and natural obstructions such as trees and undulating terrains.

Since the terrain is seldom uniform and the forces causing the wind movement are continuously changing, the wind speed is variable and could even become turbulent under certain conditions. Thus the wind-speed spectrum usually consists of many short-duration gusts.

Wind data at a region are necessary to estimate the probable wind load on new buildings. Wind speeds are measured by anemometers and the response of the instrument should be small enough to record 3-s gusts. The meteorological departments in many countries are usually responsible for the collection of wind data, and the wind speed is usually recorded at a height of 10 m above ground level on an open land site. Based on the wind data, the 3-s gust wind speed, which is likely to occur not more than once in fifty years is computed as the basic wind speed in formulating design wind speeds for buildings. In the United Kingdom the basic wind speed data have been produced by the Building Research Establishment (BRE) on the information provided by the Meteorological Office.

5.2.1. *Design Wind Speed V_s*

The design wind speed V_s for a locality may be obtained by using the basic wind speed V for the locality. The design wind speed V_s is given by the expression

$$V_s = V \times S_1 \times S_2 \times S_3$$

where S_1, S_2, and S_3, respectively, are coefficients which reflect the following parameters: (1) the topographic influence of the site location; (2) the ground roughness, gust duration relevant to the size of the building and height of structural component above ground; and (3) the expected life span of the building.

A detailed exposition of assessing wind load using the above coefficients is given by Newberry and Eaton [5.2].

In unobstructed areas, the wind speed increases with height above the ground level, and is found to obey approximately

$$V_h/V_{10} = \left(\frac{h}{10}\right)^{0.085}$$

where V_h = 3-s gust wind speed at height h metres above ground level and V_{10} = 3-s gust wind speed at 10 m height above ground level.

5.2.2. *Wind Load*

When wind is completely brought to rest by an obstacle, all the kinetic energy of the wind is transformed into dynamic pressure head q given by

$$q = \frac{\rho V_s^2}{2g}$$

where ρ = specific gravity of air, V_s = design wind speed, and g = acceleration due to gravity.

In SI units, $q = 0.613 V_s^2$ (in N/m^2) where V_s is in m/s.

Use of Fig. 5.1 facilitates the conversion of wind speed to dynamic pressure.

The air flow on striking a building is not completely stopped, but the flow pattern is changed depending on the configuration of the building. From wind tunnel experiments, it has been found possible to estimate wind pressure p for different geometric shapes of buildings, using wind pressure coefficients to modify the dynamic pressure head q. Thus

$$p = C_{p_e} \cdot q$$

where C_{p_e} denotes the pressure coefficient to determine the external pressure. Similarly, internal pressure can be estimated by using C_{p_i}, the pressure coefficient to determine the internal pressure in a cladded building.

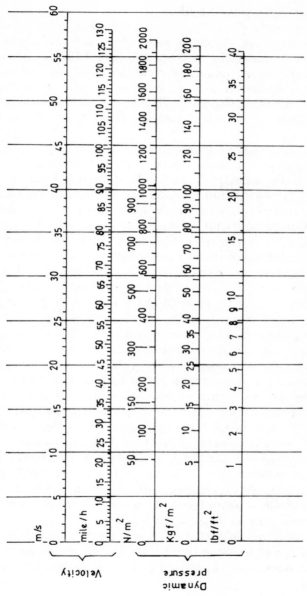

Fig. 5.1. Conversion chart for wind speed and dynamic pressure.

5.2.3. *Air Flow Around Buildings*

The pattern of air flow around buildings is influenced by many factors, chief among them being orientation of the building and wind direction in relation to adjoining buildings, plan form of the building and its height in relation to adjoining buildings, roughness of the terrain (such as hedges, trees, or for example the influence of surrounding buildings) and architectural features (for example, a projecting cantilever could modify the air flow).

5.2.4. *Wind Loads on Wall Claddings*

The pressure distributions on buildings have been found to vary with the geometry of the buildings, such as height-to-width and length-to-width ratios. Even for an isolated building, the pressure distribution on the walls are far from uniform, and vary along the height and width of the building. However, the variation of the external pressure coefficient C_{p_e}, along the height of an isolated building is relatively small compared to the variation in the horizontal direction. Thus, from wind-tunnel tests, it has been possible to establish average pressure coefficient C_{p_e} values for the four faces of a rectangular building for wind blowing on one face. Table 5.1, reproduced from the BSI Standards Code of Practice [5.1], gives the external pressure coefficient C_{p_e} for wind blowing at 90° and 0° to one face of rectangular buildings of different height-to-width and length-to-width ratios.

A noticeable phenomenon is that high suction pressures are generated at the corner regions of side walls adjoining the windward wall. The relative variation of C_{p_e} on a horizontal section of a rectangular building is illustrated in Fig. 5.2 for wind blowing normal and at an angle to one face of a building.

In order to estimate the high local suction pressures on the claddings or windows in the corner regions of buildings, the local C_{p_e} suction coefficients are given in Table 5.1. This coefficient will apply to face C of the plan form and is assumed to act for a zone width of $w/4$, as shown.

For other possible wind directions, an envelope of the worst combination of pressure coefficients C_{p_e}, can be drawn to show the maximum external pressure or suction on the claddings of a building.

Table 5.1
Pressure coefficients C_{pe} for the walls of rectangular clad buildings [5.1][a]

Building height ratio	Building plan ratio	Elevation	Plan	Wind angle, α (°)	C_{pe} for surface				Local C_{pe}
					A	B	C	D	
$\frac{h}{w} \le \frac{1}{2}$	$1 < \frac{l}{w} \le \frac{3}{2}$			0	+0·7	−0·2	−0·5	−0·5	−0·8
				90	−0·5	−0·5	+0·7	−0·2	
	$\frac{3}{2} < \frac{l}{w} < 4$			0	+0·7	−0·25	−0·6	−0·6	−1·0
				90	−0·5	−0·5	+0·7	−0·1	
$\frac{1}{2} < \frac{h}{w} \le \frac{3}{2}$	$1 < \frac{l}{w} \le \frac{3}{2}$			0	+0·7	−0·25	−0·6	−0·6	−1·1
				90	−0·6	−0·6	+0·7	−0·25	
	$\frac{3}{2} < \frac{l}{w} < 4$			0	+0·7	−0·3	−0·7	−0·7	−1·1
				90	−0·5	−0·5	+0·7	−0·1	
$\frac{3}{2} < \frac{h}{w} < 6$	$1 < \frac{l}{w} \le \frac{3}{2}$			0	+0·8	−0·25	−0·8	−0·8	−1·2
				90	−0·8	−0·8	+0·8	−0·25	
	$\frac{3}{2} < \frac{l}{w} < 4$			0	+0·7	−0·4	−0·7	−0·7	−1·2
				90	−0·5	−0·5	+0·8	−0·1	

[a]h is the height to eaves of parapet, l is the greater horizontal dimension of a building and w is the lesser horizontal dimension of a building. (Reproduced from BS CP3, Part 2, Ch. V, 1972.)

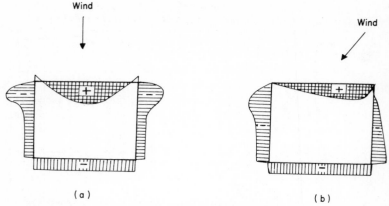

Fig. 5.2.   Variation of C_{p_e} for wind blowing (a) normal to one face and (b) at an angle to one face.

The total wind load on a window or cladding depends on the pressure difference between the outer and inner faces. If a building has openings on the windward side, then there could be internal pressures in the building owing to the air flow. Conversely, if there are openings on sides experiencing external suction, then there could be negative pressures inside the building. Thus the internal pressure in the building will depend on the degree of permeability and positions of the openings on the wind or suction faces of the wall. The BSI Code [5.1] gives some guidance on the C_{p_i} value to be used for the calculation of wind load on claddings.

An extract of the C_{p_i} coefficient given in the BSI Code [5.1] is given in Appendix 1. As an approximation, it is recommended in the Code, that when there is a small probability of a dominant opening occurring during a storm, the C_{p_i} value should be taken as the more severe of $+0.2$ and -0.3. But where a dominant opening is likely to occur, C_{p_i} should be taken as 75% of the value of C_{p_e} outside the building.

The design wind load on a window or wall cladding, of area A, is given by P where

$$P = A \cdot q \cdot (C_{p_e} - C_{p_i})$$

The $(C_{p_e} - C_{p_i})$ value is the worst combination of pressure coefficients for all probable wind directions.

It will be observed that cladding areas close to the corners of a rectangular building experience the greatest wind suction. Thus in a tall building, economy may be achieved by designing windows for the appropriate design wind loads. However, it must be borne in mind that the air flow pattern around a building could be altered when new buildings are constructed in the neighbourhood. These possibilities should be considered in the design of cladding and windows of buildings.

The following example will illustrate the method of calculating the design wind loads for windows using the BSI Code of Practice [5.1].

Example: *To determine the design wind load for the wall claddings or windows for an 18-storey building which is 55-m high and square in plan with dimensions 25 × 25 m.*

The basic wind speed for the location is 42 m/s and the building is sited in a small town. Intended life of building is to be 75 years. The design wind pressure is required for the two cases— (i) when there is negligible probability of a dominant opening occurring, and (ii) when a dominant opening is likely to occur during a storm.

Design wind speed at height 55 m:
Using Code CP3 [5.1]

S_1 factor: Table 2 $\hspace{6cm} S_1 = 1.0$
S_2 factor: Table 3
Class A, surface category 3, height 55 mm.
$$S_2 = 1.09$$
S_3 factor: Chart for S_3:
probability factor 0.63, gust not exceeding once in fifty years. Intended life of building, 75 years.
$$S_3 = 1.025$$
Design wind speed $V_s = V \times S_1 \times S_2 \times S_3$
$$= 42 \times 1.0 \times 1.09 \times 1.025$$
$$= 46.9 \text{ m/s.}$$

Corresponding dynamic pressure q is given by

$$q = 0.613 V_s^2$$
$$= 1350 \, \text{N/m}^2$$

To determine the design wind speeds at different heights, say at 40 m and at 20 m, the S_2 factors corresponding to these heights have to be adopted. Thus, the design wind speeds at 40 m and at 20 m are 42·2 m/s and 40·0 m/s, respectively.

Design wind pressure

For building height ratio $h/w = 2.2$, and building plan ratio $l/w = 1$, the C_{p_e} values are obtained from Table 5.1. The worst combination of C_{p_e} for wind blowing on face A are shown in Fig. 5.3.

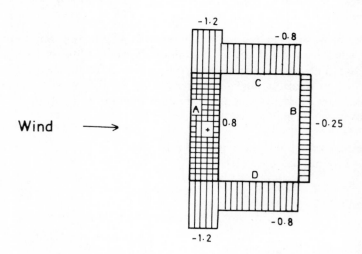

Fig. 5.3. C_{p_e} distribution for wind blowing normal to face A.

Case (i). Negligible probability of dominant opening occurring on walls.

C_{p_i} is $+0.2$ or -0.3, which ever is more severe.

The pressure on the wall or window is the difference between the external and internal pressures. From the intensity of wind pressure as indicated by the pressure coefficients, it is easy to identify the areas of maximum wind load.

Maximum suction on wall—corner zone, $p = q[-1\cdot2 - (+0\cdot2)]$
$$= -1\cdot4q$$
other areas, $p = q[-0\cdot8 - (+0\cdot2)]$
$$= -1\cdot0q$$

Maximum pressure on wall—wall areas, $p = q[+0\cdot8 - (-0\cdot3)]$
$$= +1\cdot1q$$

Case (ii). Likelihood of a dominant opening occurring.

$$C_{p_i} \text{ is } 75\% \text{ of } C_{p_e}$$

Maximum suction on wall—corner zone, $p = q[-1\cdot2 - (\tfrac{3}{4} \times 0\cdot8)]$
$$= -1\cdot8q$$
other areas, $p = q[-0\cdot8 - (\tfrac{3}{4} \times 0\cdot8)]$
$$= -1\cdot4q$$

Maximum pressure on wall—all areas, $p = q[+0\cdot8 - (-\tfrac{3}{4} \times 1\cdot2)]$
$$= +1\cdot7q$$

The calculated design wind pressures (N/m^2) on the claddings/windows are

	Case (i)			Case (ii)		
	suction		pressure	suction		pressure
	corner[a] zone	other areas	all areas	corner zone	other areas	all areas
Design wind pressure	$-1\cdot4q$	$-1\cdot0q$	$+1\cdot1q$	$-1\cdot8q$	$-1\cdot4q$	$+1\cdot7q$
Design wind pressure						
at height 55 m	$-1\,890$	$-1\,350$	$+1\,485$	$-2\,430$	$-1\,890$	$+2\,295$
at height 40 m	$-1\,753$	$-1\,252$	$+1\,377$	$-2\,254$	$-1\,753$	$+2\,128$
at height 20 m	$-1\,435$	$-1\,025$	$+1\,128$	$-1\,845$	$-1\,435$	$+1\,743$

[a] Wall length of 6·25 m from the corner.

5.3. Mechanical Properties of Ordinary Glass

In this chapter only the more important properties of glass which have a direct influence on the structural design of glass windows are discussed. A comprehensive treatment of the mechanical properties and engineering applications of glass is given by Shand [5.5].

The transparent glass types which are commonly used for windows are sheet glass, polished plate glass, and float glass. These are available only in a certain range of thicknesses. Sheet glass is available up to 6-mm thick, whereas polished plate glass is available above 6-mm thickness. Plate glass and float glass produce no distortion of vision when viewed at an angle and hence are optically superior to sheet glass, the surfaces of which are not totally parallel.

The most important properties exhibited by ordinary glass are that it is a brittle material, and that the failure strengths of glass show wide scatter. Glass is strong in compression, but weak in tension. The test results of sample glass plates [5.6] of uniform manufacture show the coefficient of variation of the failure strength to be as high as 20%.

The wide scatter in the strength of glass is attributed to the minute surface defects or imperfections present in ordinary glass. Abrasions on the surface of the glass, even invisible surface scratches, could produce stress concentrations at these surface marks when glass pane is under load. Since glass is brittle and does not yield under load, local redistribution of stress does not occur, and tensile cracks are originated at the areas of high concentration. Glaziers make use of this phenomenon to induce fracture on a chosen line by scratching the surface with a diamond or hard-surfaced stylus.

5.3.1. *Fatigue Strength of Glass*

The modulus of rupture of glass depends on the distribution and severity of flaws on the surface. The failure stress also depends on the rate of propagation of glass under loading, resulting in a higher failure strength for loads of shorter duration than for loads of longer duration. When a static load is applied to a glass pane, the flaws on the surface propagate and the glass will eventually fail at a threshold stress value, called a 'static fatigue limit'. This phenomenon of static fatigue is observed for ordinary glass under sustained loading in the presence of water vapour in the atmosphere. Typical values for the strength variation for loads of different duration based on the values given by Shand [5.5] are shown in Table 5.2. It can be seen that the breaking stress of ordinary glass under load of prolonged duration in air at room temperature is of the order of 60% of the one-minute breaking stress.

Table 5.2
Stress–time characteristics of glass tested in air[a]

Breaking stress	Duration of stress (s)						
(N/mm²)	1	3	10	60	10^2	10^4	10^6
Ordinary glass	110	101	93	80	77	58	48
	(1·37)	(1·26)	(1·16)	(1·00)	(0·96)	(0·72)	(0·60)
Tempered glass	220	215	210	202	200	183	179
	(1·09)	(1·06)	(1·04)	(1·00)	(0·99)	(0·91)	(0·89)

[a]Breaking stress values are based on curves in Shand [5.5]; values in parentheses give the breaking stress in terms of the one-minute breaking stress.

5.3.2. *Tests on Glass*

Many tests on glass have been carried out especially by glass manufacturers such as Pilkington Brothers Limited in the UK and Libbey–Owens–Ford Company in the USA, to formulate design methods for glazing. Several research workers in collaboration with the manufacturers have also conducted tests on large rectangular glass panels. The published test results of Bowles and Sugarman [5.6] on simply supported rectangular glass panes under uniformly distributed load indicate the following characteristics:

(i) Failure occurred on the tension face of the glass.
(ii) Failure of the glass panes did not always originate at the midspan region. Notably, for thicker glass panes the failure mostly originated off the midspan regions.
(iii) The failure loads depended on thickness of the glass panes.

The coefficient of variation of failure strength for each test series was of the order of 20%, whereas the coefficient of variation of maximum deflection was about 10%.

(iv) The midspan deflections at failure were much greater than the thickness of the glass panes. The mean maximum deflection for each series ranged from 1·6–8 times the thickness of the glazing for the test panel span of 1·04 m. The ratio of maximum deflection to glass thickness was higher for thinner glass panes than for thicker panes.

(v) The strain measurements on both faces of the glass pane indicated that the strains on the tension face were much greater than the strains on the compression face.

The above observations on the tests are indicative of the behaviour of glass panes under uniformly distributed load. The general conclusions from the test results are that the failure strength of ordinary glass window panes cannot be completely explained by simple bending theory based on small deflections. Because of the wide variations in the failure load, the safe strength of glass panes has to be assessed from statistical probability based on test data.

5.3.3. *Tempered Glass*

When ordinary glass is heated above its annealing range and cooled rapidly, tempered glass, which is about three to four times stronger than ordinary glass, is obtained. During the process of making this toughened glass, compressive stresses at the outer cross-section and smaller tensile stresses at the centre region are locked in. The prestressed outer surface of this glass is under compressive stress which is reliable and unaffected by surface flaws. Toughened glass which is more expensive than ordinary glass, is used in windows when extra high strength is required.

5.4. DESIGN OF WINDOW GLAZING

The deflection of a glass pane under wind load has to be limited for the safety of the window and for weather-proofing of the joints. Since the deflection is small under normal wind load conditions, the bending stress in the glass pane can be estimated using plate bending analysis. The failure load is assessed from sample tests, and the failure stress is taken as the calculated modulus of rupture of test samples assuming linear elastic behaviour till failure.

The glazing materials in glass windows usually provide varying degrees of elasticity to accommodate movement of the glass panes. For the purpose of analysis of glass panes, the edges can be conservatively assumed to be simply supported with the corners prevented from uplift. Values obtained by rigorous elastic analysis [5.9] or Marcus' formula [5.10], which is applicable to rectangular slabs for this edge condition may be used to calculate the maximum bending stress in glass panes. The maximum bending stress f by Marcus' formula is given by

$$f = (0\cdot75\ W/h^2)\left[1 - \tfrac{5}{6}\frac{r^2}{1+r^4}\right]\left[\frac{r(1+\sigma r^2)}{1+r^4}\right]$$

where W = total load on the glass pane, h = thickness of the glass pane, r = ratio of shorter side to longer side of glass pane, and σ = Poisson's ratio for glass and equals approximately $0\cdot21$ for ordinary glass.

Since the failure of glass panes does not necessarily originate at midspan, the analytical formula which gives the maximum bending stress at midspan would slightly overestimate the modulus of rupture. However, this analytical method provides a basis for a simple design method to estimate the glass thickness for glazing for a given design load.

The design bending stress is taken as the mean modulus of rupture of test samples of uniform manufacture divided by a design factor which for normal glazing is taken as 2·5. This design bending stress may be taken as $40\ \text{N/mm}^2$ for ordinary glass under 6-mm thickness, and $26\ \text{N/mm}^2$ for plate glass and float glass over 6-mm thickness.

Using the accepted safe dispersion coefficient of 25% for the strength variation, the probability of failure of glass for a design factor of 2·5 for loads below the design breaking strength, is 1 in 125. The predicted probability of failure for other design factors are given in Table 5.3.

Table 5.3
Design factor and corresponding predicted probability
of failure

Design factor	Predicted failure probability[a]
2·5	0·008 33 (1 in 120)
3·0	0·003 85 (1 in 260)
5·0	0·000 69 (1 in 1450)
7·5	0·000 27 (1 in 3700)

[a] Probability of failure of glass panes for loads below corresponding design strength.

Glass is a brittle material, and therefore when it fails there is no prior warning of impending failure. Apart from wind load stresses, induced stresses owing to thermal effects, construction methods and likely accidental loads, have to be taken into account if they are of consequence. For structures of considerable importance, higher design factors greater than 2·5 are desirable to take into consideration of all likely adverse loading conditions.

5.4.1. *Additional Limit States for Consideration*

The failure strength of glass is variable, depending on the intensity of wind load, and the duration of the load. This phenomenon of 'static fatigue' has been discussed in Section 5.3.1. The strength characteristics of glass and wind fluctuations are both complex, and a more rational method is one which can, within limits, estimate the factor of safety under service loads.

Wind loads can be considered as uniformly distributed static loads on window panes, as window panes usually have a higher natural frequency than wind flutter. Khan [5.8] recommends the following approximate method of determining the natural frequency of vibration f, given by

$$f = (17·6/\sqrt{d})\, H_3$$

where d = maximum deflection (mm) of glass under self weight.

A comprehensive design analysis of glass panes for wind loads should therefore ensure safety against extreme wind pressure that is likely to occur at least once in 50 years, and wind pressure of long duration which could cause 'fatigue failure' in glass.

The objective of the design can best be illustrated by Fig. 5.4, which gives a desired factor of safety for the strength of

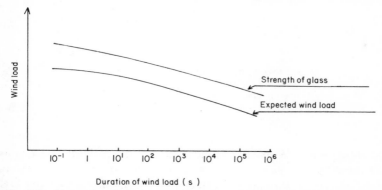

Fig. 5.4. Illustration of designed glass strength against expected wind load to ensure a desired factor of safety.

glass to resist expected wind load during the life of the building.

There is no simple relationship between wind speed and averaging time. The wind speed is a function of turbulence and varies from site to site. The 'safety factor' on the design based on a 3-s gust wind load, and one-minute breaking strength of glass, is illustrated by an example in Table 5.4. The wind speed variation with averaging time from 3 s to 1 h is used in Table 5.4 based on figures given by Lawson and Penwarden [5.11] for a site with variation of turbulence of 28%. For the variations of wind speed and breaking strength of glass indicated, the safety factor based on the design strength is 1·26, which is a reasonable value and justifies the choice of 3-s gust wind as design wind load, and one-minute breaking strength as design strength of glass. But it should be noted that wind of low turbulence, in extreme cases, may make this 'factor of safety' less than one. However, in order to estimate the overall factor of safety on the design of glazing, the design wind loads averaged over periods up to 10^6 s, along with the probability of their occurrence would be required.

Table 5.4
Illustration of safety factor on design based on 3-s gust
wind as design wind load and one-minute breaking
strength as design strength of glass, for load duration
from 3 s to 1 h

	Averaging time			
	3 s	1 min	15 min	1 h
Average wind speed [5.11] / 3-s gust wind speed	1·00	0·79	0·59	0·59
Mean breaking strength of ordinary glass / 1-min breaking strength	1·26	1·00	0·83	0·77
Partial safety factor on wind load	1·26	1·27	1·40	1·30

Mayne and Walker [5.7] have carried out a detailed analysis of the response of glazing to wind pressure on a selected site in UK. Based on this project study they have shown that the UK Glazing Code [5.3] gives a close estimate of the likely peak effective pressure on the glazing, based on the 3-s gust velocity, and that the strength of glass panes estimated by a steadily increasing load tested to failure in approximately one minute takes into account the fatigue effects of glass. However, they have indicated that the glass strength based on the one-minute test loading may not satisfy completely fatigue loads caused by high winds of low turbulence, which may occur at exposed sites.

Research efforts are being directed to formulate a simplified set of procedures encompassing all the limit states discussed for the design of glazing. Within the limit of present knowledge of glazing design, the British Glazing Code CP152: 1972 [5.3] provides a satisfactory basis of design, subject to the checking of the design for (i) fatigue limit of glass for the type of wind loading, and (ii) likely accidental loads.

5.4.2. *Design of Glazing Thickness Using the British Glazing Code CP152: 1972 [5.3]*

In this Code the procedure for calculation of design wind speed has been simplified. The design wind load is obtained by converting the wind speed to dynamic pressure, and again

multiplying by a pressure coefficient value of 1·5. This procedure could be conservative for all façade areas except for the
corner regions. A more accurate method of estimating the wind
load obtained using the BSI Code of Practice [5.1] was discussed fully in Section 5.2.

The design procedure for the calculation of glazing thickness
by the Code method can be summarised in the following steps:

Step 1: calculation of wind load:
Determine the maximum wind loading using appropriate pressure coefficients for 3-s gust wind likely to be exceeded not
more than once in 50 years.

Step 2: calculation of glass factor:
The glass factor is defined as the ratio of the area of the glass
pane to the perimeter

$$\text{Glass factor} = ab/2(a + b)$$

where a and b are the dimensions (mm) of the rectangular
window pane.

Step 3: selecting suitable glass thickness:
Table 5.5 which is reproduced from Table 5 of CP152:1972 [5.3]
is used. Wind loading is first chosen corresponding to the
calculated wind loading or equal to the next higher wind loading
in the Table. Glazing thickness corresponding to the calculated
glass factor or the next higher value is chosen.

The procedure for the design of glazing thickness in the
Code CP152:1972 revision has been simplified to contain only
one table for the design of single glazing. This is possible since
tests show that for the range of thicknesses available there are
no appreciable differences in strengths between sheet and float
glasses or between plate and float glasses of the same thickness.

The variation in design thickness obtained by using Marcus'
formula and by the Code for a given window area of varying
width-to-length ratios is shown in Fig. 5.5 by a numerical example. It is seen that for a given design wind load, the glazing

Table 5.5
Glass factors for transparent glass for single glazing[a]

Nominal glass thickness (mm)	Design wind loading (N/m²)								
	500	1 000	1 500	2 000	2 500	3 000	3 500	4 000	5 000
3	360	250	210	180	160	150	140	130	110
4	490	350	280	250	220	200	190	170	160
5	640	450	370	320	280	260	240	230	200
6	760	540	440	380	340	310	290	270	240
10	1 070	750	620	530	480	440	400	380	340
12	1 290	910	740	640	580	530	490	450	410
15	1 620	1 140	930	810	720	660	610	570	510

[a] Reproduced from BS CP152:1972, Table 5. The factors are applicable to ordinary single windows, to both glazings of any double-window systems in which both windows are openable, and to the inner glass of any form of double glazing in which the cavity is permanently vented to the outside, including most coupled windows. Up to 6-mm thick polished plate glass is no longer supplied and experimental work has shown that there is no significant difference in design strength between float and sheet glass in these thicknesses. The same glass factors can, therefore, be used for both. Sheet glass is not supplied above 6-mm thickness. In this thickness range it has been found that float and polished plate glass equate closely in design strength, so again a single set of glass factors can be used.

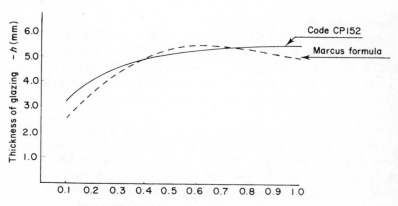

Fig. 5.5. Comparison of glass thickness obtained by BSI Code of Practice [5.3] and Marcus's formula [5.10] for a window of given area and given wind loading. Area of window, 1·5 m²; design wind loading, 2500 N/m²; design glass stress *f*, 40 N/mm².

thicknesses for windows of equal area, do not differ much for a ratio of sides ranging from 0·4 to 1·0.

Example: To design the glazing thicknesses for windows of size 1000 × 500 mm for an 18-storey building for which the wind loads have been calculated in Section 5.2.4.

Using CP152:1972

$$\text{Glass factor} = 1500 \times 1000/2(1500 + 1000) = 300$$

Design wind pressures for the building at different heights have been worked out in Section 5.2.4.

Design wind pressures in Table 5.5 closest to design wind pressures worked out are

Case (i). When there is negligible probability of a dominant opening occurring during a storm.

		Design wind pressure (N/m^2)
At height 55 m:	corner zone	2 000
	other areas	1 500
At height 40 m:	corner zone	2 000
	other areas	1 500
At height 20 m:	all areas	1 500

Case (ii). When a dominant opening is likely to occur during a storm.

	Design wind pressure (N/m^2)
At height 55 m: all areas	2 500
At height 40 m: all areas	2 500
At height 20 m: all areas	2 000

For glass factor of 300 and for wind loadings of 1500, 2000 and 2500 N/m^2, the corresponding glass design thicknesses are 5, 5 and 6 mm, respectively. Hence for case (i), the minimum glass size for all windows should be 5 mm, and for case (ii) the minimum glass size for windows above 20-m height should be 6 mm, and for windows below 20-m height, the minimum thickness should be 5 mm.

5.5. STRENGTH OF WINDOW FRAMES AND ASSEMBLY

The adequacy of structural performance of window frames and mullions is usually taken for granted. However, with architectural appearance dictating small-size window frames and with the present trend of use of larger window panes, it is necessary to check the structural performance of frames, mullions and transoms. In the case of frames and mullions, the strength is not as critical as the stiffness of the sections to prevent excessive deformation and warping. In window failures, it is not uncommon to see bent mullions and broken fixings caused by high suction pressures.

Window mullions and transoms usually have rebates on the inside so that the windows can be opened outwards. When the window is in a closed position, the wind pressure on the window is evenly transferred to the mullions and transoms. However, for suction loads, which are normally greater than wind pressure, the window has to be kept 'stayed by' the hinges and latches. The British Standards Institution [5.4] recommends that the maximum deflection for the window glass supports should be limited to 1/125 of the span for the design load corresponding to a 3-s gust wind. For double-glazed sealed units it is recommended to a limitation of 1/175 of the span, thus allowing smaller deflection for double-glazed windows [5.4].

The minimum cross-sectional size for window-frame members, mullions and transoms, capable of resisting wind loads corresponding to a 3-s gust wind, and to limit deflection to 1/125 span, can be calculated using structural analysis. The maximum bending moment in the member divided by the appropriate allowable bending stress for the material, gives the minimum section modulus for the member. For steel, the maximum stress corresponds to the yield stress of 246 N/mm^2 and for aluminium alloy HE9-WP, the 0·1% proof stress may be assumed as 154 N/mm^2. The limitation of deflection imposes a minimum size for the overall structural depth of the members, depending on the maximum extreme fibre stress in the material. Table 5.6 gives the span-to-depth ratios of idealised members to limit deflections to 1/125 span when the extreme fibre stress reaches yield/proof stress. Numerical values are given for sections

Table 5.6
Span-to-depth ratios to limit deflection of members under uniformly distributed loading

Idealised beam form	General expression for deflection for uniform beams[a]	Span-to-depth ratios to limit deflection to 1/125 span, when f corresponds to proof/yield stresses	
		aluminium alloy HE9-WP	steel
Simply supported beam			
Beam encastered at both	$l/2d_1 = 4 \cdot 8E/f \cdot \Delta/l$	16	31
ends	$l/2d_1 = 16E/f \cdot \Delta/l$	54	102
Propped cantilever	$l/2d_1 = (11-6)E/f \cdot \Delta/l$	39	74
Cantilever	$l/2d_1 = 2E/f \cdot \Delta/l$	6·8	13

[a] l is the span of beam; d_1 is the greater of the two extreme fibre distances from axis of bending, at any section; f is the maximum bending stress in material; E is Young's modulus for the material; Δ is the maximum deflection of the member.

symmetrical about the axis of bending. If the extreme fibre stresses are lower than the yield stress/proof stress, then the span-to-depth ratio will be larger than indicated in Table 5.6, though now the load capacity of the member will be reduced.

The structural members of window assembly cannot be classed as freely supported nor perfectly fixed at ends. Partial end fixity, even in the case of window types which can be opened, may justify adopting an overall depth for members supported at ends, corresponding to in-between values as given in Table 5.6 for simply supported beams and encastered beams. The maximum deflection for the window frame is related to the span of the glass pane, and hence the span lengths of the equivalent end-supported members and cantilevers have to be modified accordingly to obtain the span/depth ratios from the table. The safe span lengths of cantilevers will serve as a guide to determine the position of latches and other fixing devices for window frames. For large window assembly, closed sections such as box or tube for the members compared to open sections, will give greatest rigidity along with least torsional deformation for the assembly. Covering large areas with glazing as in the case of the Sydney Opera House are specialised projects for which detailed investigations both theoretical and experimental, are required. The final design evolved for the Sydney Opera House [5.13] uses laminated glass as the glazing material with steel tubular mullions to support the glass frames.

5.5.1. *Wind Buffeting and Other Foreseeable Loads*

Open windows, especially side-hung windows, stayed in position by stay-rods at the lower end, may have large warping deformation at the top unsupported corner when subjected to gale-force winds. The support restraints and joint-deformation characteristics are unknown factors and the stiffness of the window can best be ascertained by tests for this condition. Beckett and Godfrey [5.12] suggest the following loading test for the UK to check the stiffness of windows for wind buffeting: the test window is fixed horizontally with three corners clamped, and load is applied vertically at the free corner. The load supported for a limiting deflection of 1/20 of the offset distance from the hinge line to the load point, gives an indication of the stiffness from which the maximum wind load that it could resist safely can be estimated. A window is classed as unsafe if the maximum load it can sustain is less than 110 N.

In high-rise buildings it is possible that window-cleaners, under emergency could hang on to windows for support. This is a foreseeable type of accidental load, and different countries adopt different specification to ensure safety. The British proposal [5.12] is that windows should satisfy the following test loadings: (i) windows and hinges should not show damage for 500 N load applied for one minute at the corner; and (ii) windows should hold on without the hinges and frame giving way for a load of 1000 N applied at the outer corner.

Only the more important aspects of loadings associated with the safety of windows have been discussed and the description has been confined to the structural aspects of frames, mullions, and transoms. For detailed information on the design and construction aspects of windows, the readers should refer to Beckett and Godfrey [5.12].

ACKNOWLEDGEMENTS

The following have been reproduced by kind permission of the British Standards Institution, 2 Park Street, London W1A 2BS from whom complete copies can be obtained: Table 5.1 and Appendix 5.1 [5.1]; Table 5.5 [5.3].

APPENDIX: EXTRACT FROM CP3 [5.1] FOR THE ASSESSMENT OF C_{p_i} PRESSURE COEFFICIENT INSIDE A BUILDING

The following examples indicate approximately the values of C_{p_i} that apply to a building with a reasonably open interior plan and are to be applied to the same values of q as the building in which they occur. If the interior is divided by relatively impermeable partitions the pressure difference between windward and leeward faces of the building will be broken down in steps, and will impose loads on the partitions.

(1) *Two opposite faces equally permeable; other faces impermeable*
   (a) wind normal to permeable face, $C_{p_i} = +0\cdot2$
   (b) wind normal to impermeable face, $C_{p_i} = -0\cdot3$
(2) *Four faces equally permeable,* $C_{p_i} = -0\cdot3$
(3) *With equal permeability on all faces except for a dominant opening on one or other face, of size and position as follows:*
   (a) on windward face, making the permeability of the windward face equal to the following proportions of the total distributed permeability of all the faces subject to suction.
   Proportion 1, $C_{p_i} = +0\cdot1$
   Proportion $1\frac{1}{2}$, $C_{p_i} = +0\cdot3$

Proportion 2, $C_{p_i} = +0\cdot5$
Proportion 3 or more, $C_{p_i} = +0\cdot6$
(b) on leeward face: any dominant opening, $C_{p_i} = -0\cdot3$
(c) on a face parallel to the wind
   (i) any dominant opening not in an area of high local C_{p_e}, $C_{p_i} = -0\cdot4$
   (ii) in an area of high local C_{p_e}:
       if the area of the opening equals the following proportion of the total other distributed permeability of all the external faces subject to suction
       $\frac{1}{4}$ or less, $C_{p_i} = -0\cdot4$
       $\frac{1}{2}$, $C_{p_i} = -0\cdot5$
       $\frac{3}{4}$, $C_{p_i} = -0\cdot6$
       1, $C_{p_i} = -0\cdot7$
       $1\frac{1}{2}$, $C_{p_i} = -0\cdot8$
       3 or more, $C_{p_i} = -0\cdot9$

The distributed permeability should be assessed in each case as accurately as is practicable. As a guide it can be said that the typical permeability of a house or office block with all windows nominally closed is in the range of $0\cdot01$–$0\cdot05\%$ of the face area, depending on the degree of draught-proofing.

Where it is not possible, or is not considered justified, to estimate the value of C_{p_i} for a particular case, the coefficient should be based on one of the following for any determination of wall or roof loading: (1) where there is only a negligible probability of a dominant opening occurring during a severe storm, C_{p_i} should be taken as the more onerous of $+0\cdot2$ and $-0\cdot3$; (2) for situations where a dominant opening is likely to occur, C_{p_i} should be taken as 75% of the value of C_{p_e} outside the opening. The extreme conditions should be determined for the various wind directions that give rise to critical loadings and it should be noted that especially severe internal pressures may be developed if a dominant opening is located in a region of high local external pressure.

Chapter 6

Acoustic Behaviour of Windows

The Mass law is briefly described, and the various types of windows commonly used in the tropics are illustrated and their acoustic properties explained.

The acoustic properties of single-glazed and double-glazed windows are well known. The initial development of these windows has been due to the need to increase the thermal properties of windows in countries with temperate climates. The introduction of thicker plate glass, double glazing, and air tightness of glazing prevents the loss of heat to the outside. In doing so, the windows also gain good acoustic qualities as the attenuation of sound due to these measures is better than that of ordinary single sheet. However, in the tropics, these methods are only applicable to air-conditioned buildings, as the means to prevent heat gain are equally applicable to heat loss. In buildings where air-conditioning is not used, windows are opened for ventilation. There is little insulation against intruding noise. It is therefore important for the designer to consider the acoustic properties of open windows, their location and the general planning of the estate so as to minimise noise intrusion and to provide a better acoustic environment.

6.1. THE ACOUSTIC BEHAVIOUR OF WINDOWS

The two most important contributions to good sound insulation properties are *mass* and *air-tightness*.

6.1.1. *Mass Law*

Most of the principles involved in direct sound transmission are illustrated by considering a single-leaf wall. Acoustic wave motion may be shown to be transmitted through air as a succession of compressions and rarefactions travelling in the direction of propagation of the sound waves, at about 330 m/s. In other words, air is able to transmit longitudinal wave motion by virtue of its compressibility.

A wall, however, is constructed from an incompressible material and as such it cannot transmit acoustic wave motion in the manner of the surrounding air. Figure 6.1 shows how an

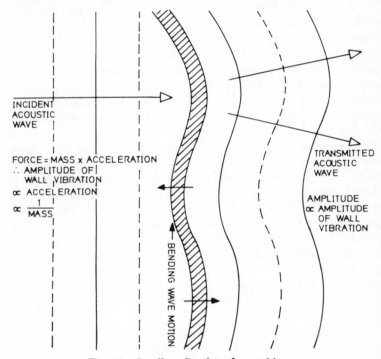

Fig. 6.1.   Bending vibration of a partition.

incident sound wave acts on the partition and, through its pressure fluctuations, sets it into flexible or bending movements. Though these movements have extremely small magnitude, they radiate sound from the opposite side of the partition and also set the supporting structural members into vibration.

The amplitude of the sound waves radiating into the receiving room depends only on the amplitude of vibrations in the wall and not on any other properties of the wall. The amplitude of the wall vibrations in turn depends on the amplitude of the pressure oscillations in the source room which acts on the wall.

In an oscillatory system, amplitude and acceleration are proportional to one another. Applying Newton's Second Law of Motion it can thus be seen that the amplitude of wall vibrations is inversely proportional to the mass of the wall. It follows therefore that the amplitude of sound waves radiated into the receiving room is similarly inversely proportional to the mass of the wall.

Sound is energy, and sound transmission is measured in terms of the energy reaching the receiving room. Since energy is proportional to the square of velocity, and thus to the square of the amplitude, the transmitted sound is inversely proportional to the square of the mass of the wall. This means that by doubling the mass of the wall, sound transmission is reduced by one-quarter. In terms of decibels, the insulation is increased by $10 \log_{10} 4 \simeq 6 \, \text{dB}$. By applying the same reasoning, it can be shown that a doubling in frequency will also produce a 6-dB increase in sound insulation. These statements about the effects of changes in mass and frequency constitute the Mass law. This is quantified in Fig. 6.2 where the average sound reduction indices of solid partitions are plotted against their weight per

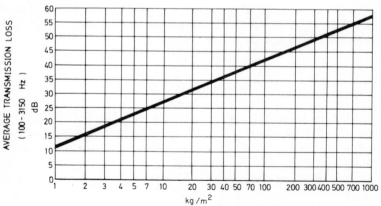

Fig. 6.2. Mass law.

unit area. It will be seen that, in general, there is an increase in insulation of about 5 dB for each doubling of weight.

The insulation from a single partition is approximately

$$R_{av} = 10 + 14 \cdot 5 \log_{10} m$$

where R_{av} = average sound reduction (dB), and m = mass per unit area (kg/m²). The greater the mass, the larger the insulation provided by a partition. A brick wall, 230-mm (9-in.) thick, has a mass of 415 kg/m² and gives an average sound insulation of about 50 dB. The use of mass up to that of the brick wall is often the most economical method of providing sound insulation. However, above an average of 50 dB, other methods must be considered. In some cases, structural considerations may prevent the use of mass to provide even moderate sound insulation.

6.1.2. *Air-Tightness*

The second important consideration is that the barrier or partition should be completely sealed so that there are no air passages through which sound can easily be transmitted to short-circuit the resistance of the barrier. Even very narrow gaps, such as may occur in the mortar joints of poorly constructed brickwork, cause a significant reduction in sound insulation. A wall which might normally have an insulation of 50 dB would have this reduced by means of a hole of only 1/100 of the total area to about 30 dB. Thus the first consideration must be to try to raise the insulation of the poorest parts, which means that air gaps should be eliminated.

6.2. WINDOWS IN BUILDINGS

There is no single best design for a window. The occupant of a particular building, his functional requirements, his cost budget, his reliance on lighting, heating (not applicable to tropical countries like Singapore) or air-conditioning services, and his reaction to visual and climatological factors, all dictate a unique solution. The rising cost of urban sites, the need for economical utilisation of floor spaces, the increasing standards of comfort and the greater reliance on building services havé made a special contribution to creating a demand for new performance specifications for the building façade. As a consequence, in each building, different degrees of importance will be given to the daylighting, visual, thermal and acoustic performances of the window. The following discussions which deal with five principal types of window are therefore not intended as a design guide but more a description of the insulation qualities of each of them.

6.2.1. *Openable, Single Windows*

The normal, singly glazed, openable window does not possess the two important contributions to good sound insulation qualities, *i.e.* mass and air-tightness.

The mass per unit area of the glazing is usually many times less than that of the wall to which the window is mounted and the small gaps normally found around the edges of openable windows are often large enough to allow sufficient sound through to reduce the already low window insulation.

If the opening element can be closed onto an efficient, resilient seal the full insulation capability of the window can be obtained and such a window, when closed, will have an average sound insulation of about 25 dB depending on the weight of the glass. If no special provisions are made for sealing the gap around the opening element, the insulation will be lower, about 20 dB, depending on the width of the unsealed gaps. The efficiency of flexible seals is likely to deteriorate with time and there may be a consequent decrease in sound insulation.

With the opening element opened, as in Fig. 6.3, the window insulation will be very much reduced. The value will depend on the opening, the absorption properties of the room and the position of the observer. For a person near the centre of the room the insulation due to a window with an open element would be about 5–15 dB and this would fall to zero as the observer approached the open window.

The use of ventilation fans fitted with a shutter has made it possible to improve the sound insulating properties of ventilating windows. A sealed, single window fitted with a fan with an

Fig. 6.3.   Window with opening element.

efficient shutter mechanism will have a sound insulation about the same as that of an openable single window, about 30 dB, when both are in the closed position. But, in the open, ventilating position the open area required through the fan is so small that the insulation of that window is only reduced by 1 or 2 dB whereas the insulation of the window with the opening light is reduced by 10 dB or more.

6.2.2. *Sealed, Single Windows*

The insulation provided by sealed single windows, where the sealing is perfect and permanent, will depend entirely on the

Table 6.1
*Typical average insulation values for
sealed, single windows*

Thickness and weight of glass	Average insulation (dB)
3 mm (24 oz.)	24
4 mm (32 oz.)	25
6 mm ($\frac{1}{4}$ in.)	28
12 mm ($\frac{1}{2}$ in.)	33

weight of the glass. Typical average insulation values are shown in Table 6.1.

6.2.3. *Openable, Double Windows*

The sound insulation of openable, double windows depends on the weight of the glazing, the size of the gaps around the openable elements and the widths of the air space. The small air space, 6- or 12-mm wide, in sealed double-glazing units manufactured (under trade names 'Twindow', 'Thermopane', *etc.*) for thermal insulation purposes gives no advantage in sound insulation and these units should be regarded, acoustically, as single glazing of thickness equal to the total thickness of glass in the unit. There is no optimum width for the air space: the wider, the better. An air space 100-mm (4-in.) wide is generally considered to be the smallest space that gives a worthwhile improvement in sound insulation. Practical considerations often limit the width of the air space to 200–300 mm (8–12 in.) but, for good sound insulation, the aim should be to put the two leaves as far apart as possible. It is also desirable to line the window reveals with a sound absorbent material such as perforated soft fibreboard.

If both leaves have openable elements with good fit and can be closed against efficient sealing strips and if the reveals are lined with sound absorbent material, the sound insulation of openable, double windows can be as high as 40–45 dB. The maintenance of this value will depend, as for single glazing, on the permanence of the properties of the sealing strip.

The insulation provided by a double window with openable elements, as shown in Fig. 6.4(a) when both elements are open, will be about the same as that of an open single window *i.e.* 5–10 dB. If the opening elements are staggered, as in Fig. 6.4(b), and the window reveals are lined with absorbent materials with both elements open, the sound insulation may be 10–20 dB.

Figure 6.4(c) shows the schematic representation of a window with openings restricted to 75 or 100 mm (3 or 4 in.) and staggered, one at the top of one leaf, the other at the bottom of the other leaf. With absorbent lining to the air-space reveals, this system gives a sound insulation of about 25 dB, which is as good

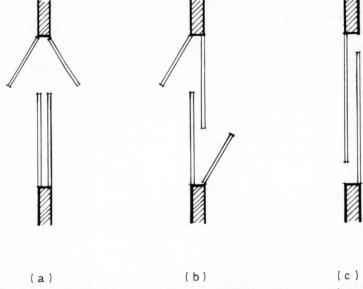

(a)   (b)   (c)

Fig. 6.4. Double glazing. (a), adjacent opening elements; (b), staggered opening elements; (c), ventilated double glazing.

as that of a sealed, single window but can allow some natural ventilation.

As in the case of the openable, single windows, shuttered ventilating fans used with double windows can provide both ventilation and a fairly high sound insulation. The fan should be placed at the top of one leaf and the ventilation gap in the other leaf should be in the diagonally opposite position. Such construction would give a sound insulation of 30 dB or more with the fan closed. With the fan open and providing ventilation the sound insulation would be about 28 dB.

6.2.4. *Non-Openable, Double Windows*

A non-openable, double window can be defined as one in which at least one leaf of the double window is permanently sealed. To obtain the highest insulation, both leaves should be sealed, the air spaces should be as wide as possible (at least 200 mm) and the reveals should be lined with sound-absorbent material. Such a window could have an insulation as high as 40–45 dB. The use of thicker glass is an advantage but the increase owing to weight is not so marked as in single windows. For sealed double windows it is preferable that each glass should be of different thickness or mass per unit area in order to eliminate acoustical coupling and resonance. These methods of increasing the sound-insulating quality of windows are used in the installation of control and observation windows in radio, TV and recording studios (Fig. 6.5).

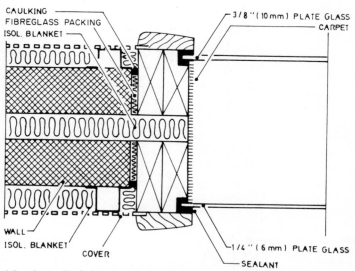

Fig. 6.5. Control window between a radio or recording studio and a sound-control room.

Unless the air space is hermetically sealed, the enclosed surfaces of the glass will need occasional cleaning and it is therefore most convenient if one leaf of the double window can be opened. If the other leaf is sealed and the gaps around the opening leaf are kept small—say 2% of the surface area would be a reasonable upper limit—the sound insulation of the window will be almost 40 dB, only slightly less than that of a fully-sealed double window.

If a still higher degree of sound insulation is expected from a window, triple-pane construction is preferable to a very thick single pane. The distance between the panes has a distinct effect on the sound insulation of the window particularly at low frequencies and the insulation improves with increasing distance between the panes. If a reasonable distance cannot be secured between the panes, it is then advisable to increase the thickness *i.e.* the weight, of the panes. Figures 6.6 and 6.7 give the range of sound insulation of single- and double-glazed windows.

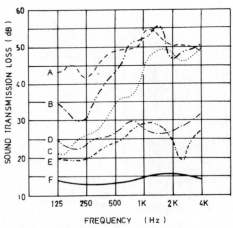

Fig. 6.6. Transmission loss values of various window constructions with weather-stripped and sealed edges: A, double window, $\frac{1}{2}$-in. (13-cm) plate glass and 8-in. (20-cm) air space; B, double window, 24-oz. (3-mm) glazings and 8-in. (20-cm) air space; C, double window, 24-oz. (3-mm) glazings and 4-in. (100-mm) air space; D, single window, $\frac{1}{2}$-in. (13-mm) plate glass; E, single window 24-oz. (3-mm) glazing; F, open window. All double windows (A, B and C) have sound-absorptive reveals. (Courtesy of McGraw-Hill Book Co. Ltd.)

6.2.5. *Louvred Windows*

As expected, louvred windows have poor transmission-loss characteristics. Measurements of reverberant-to-free-field sound insulation of such a window, having 6-mm ($\frac{1}{4}$-in.) glass panes,

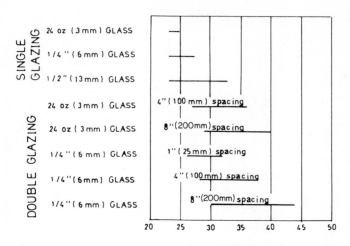

Fig. 6.7. Ranges of sound insulation of single- and double-glazed windows. Values on the left represent windows that can be opened; values on the right represent fixed windows.

have produced an average transmission loss (TL) of 22 dB for the sixteen test frequencies (100–3150 Hz), in third octaves, when fully closed and hermetically sealed. Again, as expected, the window has practically zero insulation when fully opened with the louvres maintained horizontal (Fig. 6.8).

Results of investigations on the variation of sound pressure level with vertical distance at different angles of inclination of the louvres with the vertical have shown that, with the louvres inclined, the high-frequency components (that is, wavelengths smaller than or comparable to the 'effective' width (Fig. 6.9) of the apertures formed by the louvres) of the incident noise tend to be concentrated more towards the ceiling of the room than anywhere else, provided, of course, the receiver positions are at distances (from the window) comparable to the dimensions of the window. This phenomenon is attributed chiefly to the reflections of these high-frequency components as they strike the inclined louvres.

At wavelengths greater than the width of the apertures or at

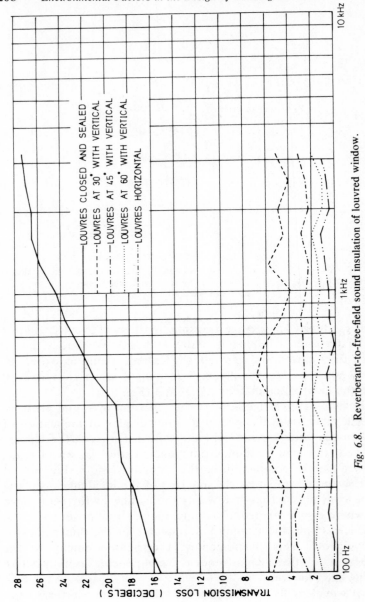

Fig. 6.8.   Reverberant-to-free-field sound insulation of louvred window.

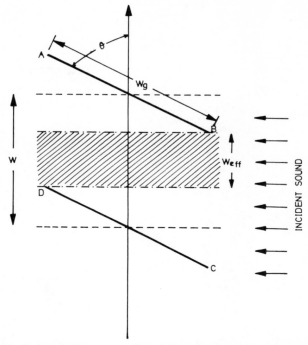

Fig. 6.9. Geometrical representation of the 'effective' width of aperture.

distances greater than the size of the window the diffraction effect predominates (this is also true even at wavelengths smaller than, or comparable to, the width of the aperture). Variations of sound pressure level with vertical distance and the angle of inclination with the vertical, θ, are shown in Figs. 6.10–6.18.

The tendency for the high-frequency sounds to be reflected towards the ceiling after striking the inclined louvres of a window is very significant as far as architectural designs of rooms are concerned, especially in the tropics (*e.g.* the Republic of Singapore) where louvred windows generally act as the link between the inside and outside. To reduce the high-frequency components of sound transmitted into a room through a louvred window, especially with the louvres inclined (and this, for the

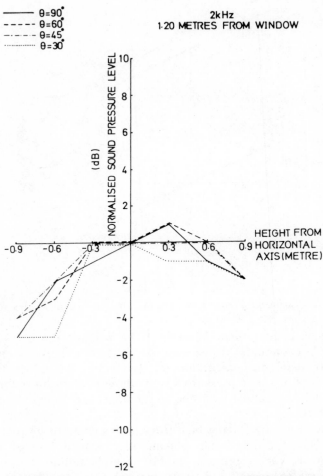

Fig. 6.10. Variation of the sound pressure level with vertical distance and the angle of inclination with the vertical, θ. See also Figs. 6.11–6.18.

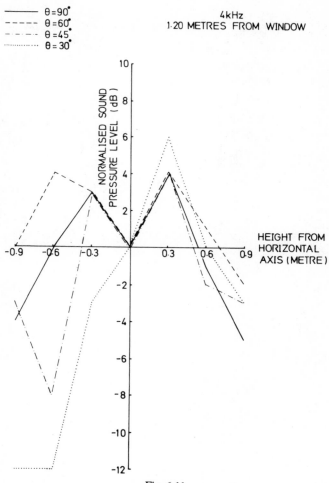

Fig. 6.11.

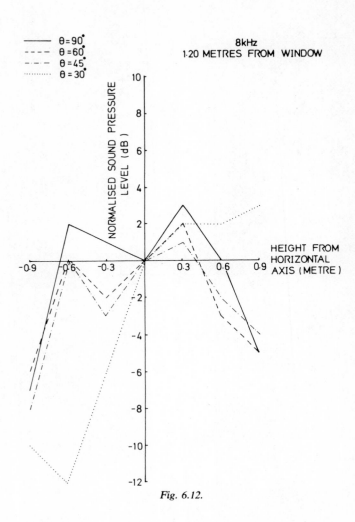

Fig. 6.12.

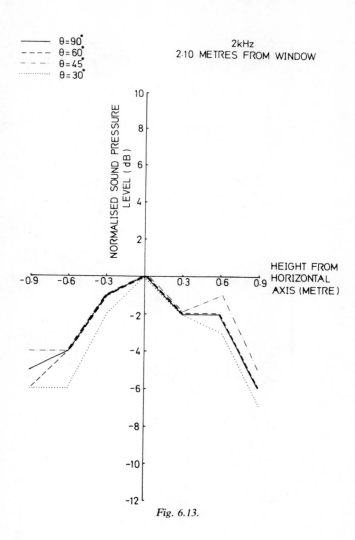

Fig. 6.13.

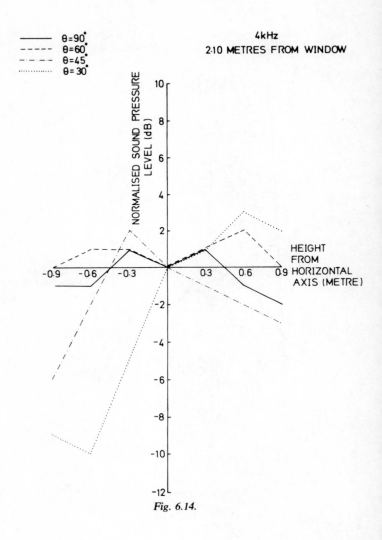

Fig. 6.14.

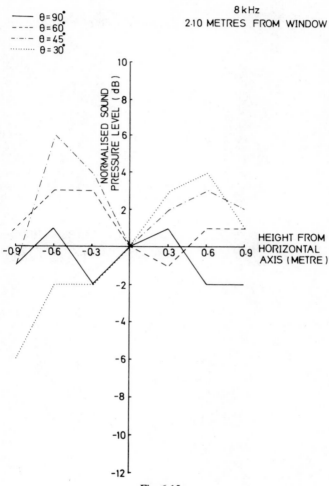

Fig. 6.15.

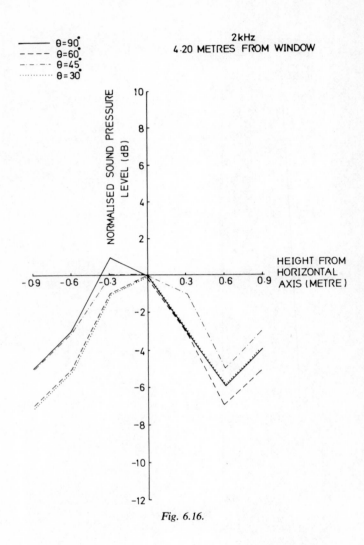

Fig. 6.16.

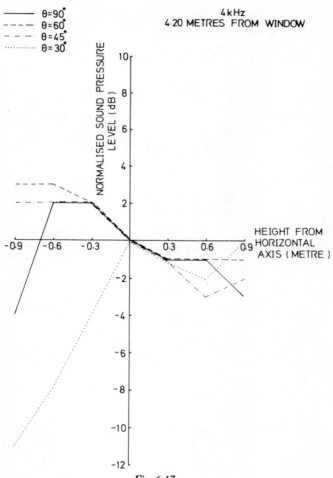

Fig. 6.17.

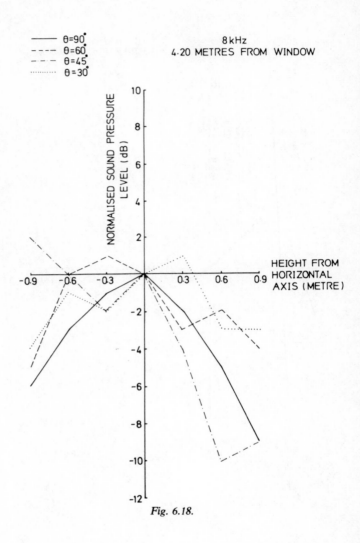

Fig. 6.18.

Table 6.2
Average insulation values for louvred and other types of window

Type of window	Average insulation (dB)
Louvred window (closed and hermetically sealed)	22
Closed, well-fitting, single window	25
Heavy (6-mm plate) single windows with edges well sealed	25–30
9–5 mm plate-glass window mounted in neoprene gasket	31
Fully treated double-glazed windows, sealed with 200-mm airspace and absorbent reveals	35–40

sake of privacy, is much preferred in Singapore than to have the louvres horizontal), one needs therefore only to ensure that that part of the ceiling which geometrically comes within the region of the reflected sounds is adequately absorbent.

For the purpose of comparing the performance of the louvred window with other types of window, Table 6.2 gives the average values of insulation for these windows.

Chapter 7

Solar Optical Properties of Glass

The reflection, absorption and transmission characteristics of glass are discussed. The mechanism of heat gain through clear glass is shown. Various solar control glasses and their application in building are illustrated. The method of calculating their shade coefficients is also shown.

7.1. INTRODUCTION

One of the characteristics of modern architecture is the use of large expanses of glass in the building façades, irrespective of the climate of the place. This has resulted in the overheating of buildings owing to excessive heat gain even in temperate climates. To overcome this problem recent advances in glass technology have succeeded in the production of special glasses with varying solar optical properties. These developments have quickly attracted architects, as they provide some form of solar control of fenestrations without necessitating the reduction of glass area. However, proper selection of the type of glass and shading devices is important for reducing the heat gains through glazed areas and thus the energy demands for maintaining indoor thermal environments at comfortable levels. To estimate the solar heat gain through different types of glasses their spectral reflection, absorption and transmission characteristics for the entire range of wavelengths of solar spectrum are required. This chapter deals with these properties of glass.

7.2. REFLECTION, ABSORPTION AND TRANSMISSION CHARACTERISTICS OF GLASS

When a beam of solar radiation is incident on a glass surface, a part is reflected, a part is absorbed by the glass and the rest is transmitted. The relative proportions of these three components

220

depend on the type of glass, thickness of the pane, and the angle of incidence. The spectral transmittance depends on the chemical composition of the glass, tint and colour and special surface coatings. In order to obtain the solar transmission and absorption characteristics of a specific glass, its reflection absorption and transmission factors for monochromatic radiation must be determined for the full range of spectral bands of solar radiation. In general, measured data on the spectral transmission for normal incidence are available for most of the common types of architectural glass. Glass manufacturers normally provide the data on their products in their technical literature. Solar spectral transmittance data of typical clear, heat-absorbing and heat-reflecting glasses, presented by Yellot [7.1] are shown in Fig. 7.1.

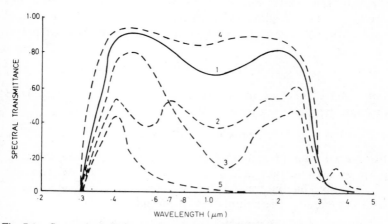

Fig. 7.1. Spectral transmittance for typical architectural glass $\frac{1}{4}$-in-thick plate. 1, Soda lime; 2, grey heat-absorbing; 3, green heat-absorbing; 4, borosilicate; 5, selective-reflectance glass. (After Yellot [7.1]).

A large variety of glasses in each type is marketed and their spectral transmission characteristics may vary to some extent.

For monochromatic radiation, the variations with angle of incidence in solar reflectance and transmittance of a glass can be derived theoretically from the normal incidence transmittance data. Parmelea [7.2], Mitalas and Stephenson [7.3], and Spencer [7.4] have dealt with this problem in more detail and derived equations from first principles of geometrical optics. The ratio of reflected to incident radiation for a single reflection at an air-glass interface is given by Fresnel's formula as

$$r = \frac{1}{2}\left[\frac{\sin^2(i-i')}{\sin^2(i+i')}\right] + \frac{1}{2}\left[\frac{\tan^2(i-i')}{\tan^2(i+i')}\right] \qquad (7.1)$$

where i and i' are the angles of incidence and refraction, respectively. The angle of refraction is obtained from Snell's law as

$$\sin i' = \frac{\sin i}{\omega} \qquad (7.2)$$

where ω is the refractive index of glass. The part that is absorbed by the glass while the beam of radiation is traversing through the glass depends on the product of extinction coefficient of the glass (k) and the path length (l) i.e. the kl value. The fraction that is transmitted is given by Lambert's law as

$$T = e^{-kl} \qquad (7.3)$$

For a glass sheet of thickness d the path length (l) traversed through the glass will be given by

$$l = d/\cos i' \quad i.e. \ d \sec i' \qquad (7.4)$$

For a glass pane of finite thickness, multiple reflections will take place at each surface as illustrated in Fig. 7.2. The net fraction of radiation finally transmitted after successive reflections is then obtained by the summation of the infinite series as

$$\tau_\tau = (1-r^2)T + r^2(1-r^2)T^3 + r^4(1-r^2)T^5 + \ldots \qquad (7.5)$$

The above series is a convergent geometric series, hence the expression for the total monochromatic transmissivity is given as

$$\tau_\lambda = \frac{(1-r^2)T}{1-r^2T^2} \qquad (7.6)$$

In a similar way we obtain the total monochromatic reflectivity as

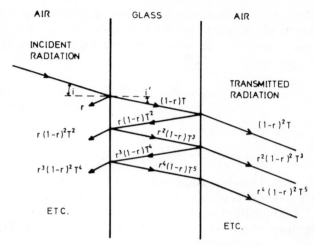

Fig. 7.2. Multiple reflection and transmission through a glass sheet of finite thickness.

$$\rho_\lambda = \frac{r + r(1 - r^2)T^2}{1 - r^2T^2} \qquad (7.7)$$

From the fact that the sum of reflected, absorbed and transmitted components is unity, the absorptivity is obtained from the reflectivity and transmissivity factors as

$$\alpha_\lambda = (1 - \rho_\lambda - \tau_\lambda) \qquad (7.8)$$

The foregoing is valid for monochromatic radiation only as the extinction coefficient (k) of a glass varies with the wavelength of the radiation. The overall transmissivity of glass for solar radiation is obtained by integration over the whole solar spectrum. If I_λ is the average relative radiation intensity in a narrow spectral band of wavelength interval of λ and $\lambda + \Delta\lambda$, and τ_λ is the corresponding transmissivity, then the overall transmission factor for solar radiation is obtained as

$$\tau = \frac{\Sigma (I_\lambda \cdot \tau_\lambda)\Delta\lambda}{\Sigma (I_\lambda \cdot \Delta\lambda)} \qquad (7.9)$$

Thus the solar transmittance of a glass at a particular angle of incidence is the weighted mean of the spectral transmittances at this angle. Similarly, the solar reflectivity (ρ) and absorptivity (α) are obtained by

$$\rho = \frac{\Sigma\,(I_\lambda \cdot \rho_\lambda)\Delta\lambda}{\Sigma\,(I_\lambda \cdot \Delta\lambda)} \qquad (7.10)$$

and

$$\alpha = \frac{\Sigma\,(I_\lambda \cdot \alpha_\lambda)\Delta\lambda}{\Sigma\,(I_\lambda \cdot \Delta\lambda)} \qquad (7.11)$$

The normal incident solar transmittance and the equivalent *kl* values for a few typical types of window glasses are given in Table 7.1. The variation of normal incidence solar transmittance as a function of the *kl* value of the glass is shown in Fig. 7.3.

Table 7.1
Normal incidence solar transmittance and equivalent kl values for a few types of glasses

Type of glass	Normal incidence solar transmittance (%)	Equivalent *kl* value
3-mm Clear sheet glass	85	0·08
6-mm Clear float glass	80	0·15
6-mm Lightly heat-absorbing glass	42	0·79
6-mm Densely heat-absorbing glass	20	1·51
6-mm Grey (anti-glare) glass	42	0·79

Stephenson [7.5] has computed the solar transmissivity and absorptivity data for the range of angles of incidence from 0 to 90° as a function of the *kl* value. The results are presented graphically in Figs. 7.4 and 7.5, respectively. Stephenson and Mitalas have further modified the calculation procedure to be more suitable for computer machine calculations by expressing the transmissivity and absorptivity as polynomials in cosine of the angle of incidence *i.e.* cos *i*. These are expressed as

$$\tau_{(i)} = \sum_{n=0}^{5} t_n \cos n_i \qquad (7.12)$$

and

$$\alpha_{(i)} = \sum_{n=0}^{5} a_n \cos n_i \qquad (7.13)$$

The values of the polynomial coefficients for transmission (t_n)

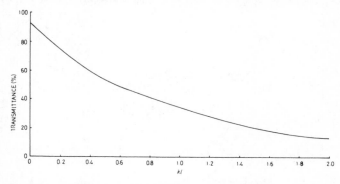

Fig. 7.3. Transmission at normal incidence as a function of *kl* product for window glass.

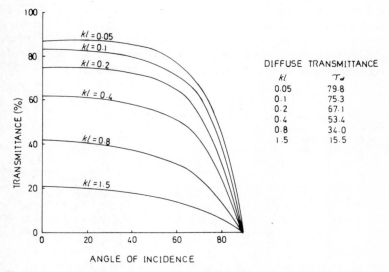

Fig. 7.4. Transmittance of glass as a function of angle of incidence and *kl* value.

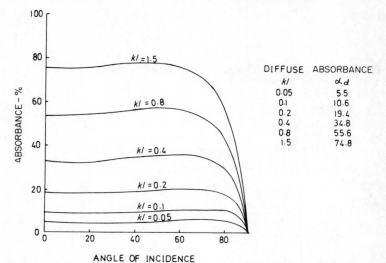

Fig. 7.5. Absorbance of glass as a function of angle of incidence and kl value.

and absorption (a_n) for clear window glass and a heat-absorbing glass are given in Table 7.2.

The transmittance and absorbance for diffuse radiation is obtained by integrating the above expressions for angles of incidences of 0 to $\pi/2$. These are thus obtained as

Table 7.2
Polynomial coefficients for absorption and transmission factors of glass

Polynomial coefficient (n)	Ordinary clear glass		Heat-absorbing glass	
	absorption (a_n)	transmission (t_n)	absorption (a_n)	transmission (t_n)
0	0·011 54	−0·008 85	0·014 06	−0·008 35
1	0·776 74	2·712 35	4·159 58	0·927 66
2	−3·946 57	−0·620 62	−15·062 79	2·157 21
3	8·578 81	−7·073 29	27·184 92	−8·714 29
4	−8·381 35	9·759 95	−23·885 18	9·871 52
5	3·011 88	−3·899 22	8·036 50	−3·733 28
Diffuse values	0·054 4	0·799 0	0·464 1	0·426 8

(After Mitalas and Stephenson [7.3])

$$\tau_{(d)} = 2 \sum_{n=0}^{5} \frac{t_n}{n+2} \qquad (7.14)$$

and

$$\alpha_{(d)} = 2 \sum_{n=0}^{5} \frac{a_n}{n+2} \qquad (7.15)$$

In the case of double glazing the transmission of each glass pane is to be found as a function of wavelength, and angle of incidence, and lastly the overall solar transmittance of the system. This can be obtained by the equation

$$\tau = \frac{\tau_1 \tau_2}{1 - \rho_1 \rho_2} \qquad (7.16)$$

where τ_1 and τ_2 are the transmittances, and ρ_1 and ρ_2 are the reflectances of first and second panes, respectively. Similarly the expressions for reflectance and absorbance for double glazing can be obtained as

$$\rho = \rho_1 + \frac{\rho_2 \tau_1^2}{1 - \rho_1 \rho_2} \qquad (7.17)$$

and

$$\alpha_1 = a_1 \left(1 + \frac{\tau_1 \rho_2}{1 - \rho_1 \rho_2} \right) \qquad (7.18)$$

$$\alpha_2 = \frac{\tau_1 a_2}{1 - \rho_1 \rho_2} \qquad (7.19)$$

It is equally important to obtain light transmission characteristics of different glazing systems, as one of the major functions of a window is to provide natural light into buildings. This can be determined by considering the visible region of the solar spectrum only.

From the foregoing it can be seen that the calculation procedures are complex and tedious. A large amount of computational effort is required to obtain solar optical properties of single and double glazed window systems. Computer programs are available [7.6] for performing these calculations. They require only the normal incidence transmittances of the glass at narrow wavelength intervals of say 10 nm. The programs calculate the transmittance reflectance and absorbance for the entire solar spectrum as well as for visible (0.38–$0.76\ \mu m$) and infrared (0.76–$2.5\ \mu m$) parts separately for all angles of incidence.

7.3. Mechanism of Heat Gain Through Clear Glass

The solar heat gain through glass includes a fraction of the absorbed energy by the glass pane that is transferred to interior space by convection and radiation, in addition to the solar transmittance *i.e.*

solar heat gain = (solar transmittance) + ($f \times$ solar absorbance)

where f is the fraction of absorbed energy that is transferred to interior space. Its value depends on the indoor and outdoor air temperatures and the wind velocity at either surfaces. Under normal conditions, a value of 0.27–0.33 is assumed. However, under conditions of still air at the outside surface this value can be nearly 0.5. The mechanism of heat gain through a clear glass is shown in Fig. 7.6.

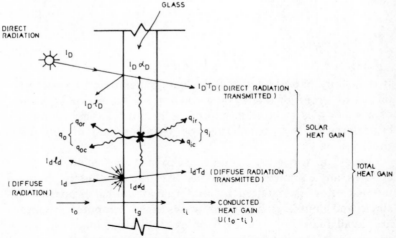

Fig. 7.6.   Mechanism of heat transfer through glass.

Table 7.3
Solar optical properties and heat:light ratios of different types of glasses

Type of glass	Solar optical properties			Total solar heat gain (%)	Daylight transmission (%)	Heat:light ratio
	reflectance (%)	absorptance (%)	transmittance (%)			
Clear glass						
3-mm sheet glass	7	8	85	87	90	0·97
6-mm float glass	8	12	80	84	87	0·96
6-mm wired glass	6	31	63	71	85	0·83
Coloured pattern glass						
3-mm green	6	55	39	56	49	1·14
3-mm blue	6	32	62	72	31	2·32
3-mm amber	6	40	52	66	58	1·14
Heat-absorbing glass						
6-mm grey glass	5	51	44	60	41	1·46
6-mm blue–green glass	5	75	20	43	48	0·85
6-mm green	6	49	45	60	75	0·80
6-mm bronze glass	5	51	44	60	50	1·20
6-mm spectral float glass (bronze)	10	34	56	66	49	1·35
Heat-reflecting glass (laminated; 6-mm gold-coated glass)						
heavy-density coating	47	42	11	25	20	1·25
medium-density coating	33	42	25	41	38	1·08
light-density coating	21	43	36	53	63	0·84

7.4. HEAT:LIGHT RATIOS

Evidently, the ideal system of window glazing is one that has considerably higher light transmission than that of the overall solar heat transmission. Hence a useful criteria for the performance of glass is the heat:light transmission ratio [7.6]. Glasses that reduce solar heat gain more than light will have ratios of less than unity. This is the class of glasses that selectively absorbs the infrared part of the solar spectrum. On the other hand, glasses that absorb more in the visible part of the solar spectrum have heat:light ratios greater than unity. The solar optical properties, solar heat gain, light transmission and heat:light ratios of a number of window glass types at normal incidence are given in Table 7.3.

It can be seen from Table 7.3 that, as a rule, heat-absorbing glasses have a better heat:light ratio index. The lightly heat-absorbing glass is better in this respect than that of the densely heat-absorbing glass. Clear glass also has a ratio of less than unity. Tinted and coloured glasses popularly known as anti-glare glasses, on the other hand have heat:light ratios greater than unity *i.e.* admit more solar heat than light transmission.

7.5. DAILY MEAN SOLAR TRANSMITTANCES

As the solar transmittances of glass are a function of the angle of incidence, the solar heat gains through glazed windows vary with the time of day, month, orientation of the window elevation, latitude of the place and also the radiation regime of the locality. However, the concept of daily mean solar transmittance, which is in effect the weighted-mean transmittance for the window glass, simplifies the procedure for determining the daily mean solar heat gain and the calculation of mean rise in indoor air temperature. The daily mean transmittances are obtained by integrating the hourly solar heat gains over the day and expressing them as a ratio of the daily total of incident solar radiation on the glass. Evidently, the daily mean transmittances will vary with orientation and time of the year at any place. To illustrate the range of variation, these values for different orientations for a clear day in each month are calculated for Singapore and presented in Tables 7.4 and 7.5.

Table 7.4
Daily mean solar transmittances of clear glass^a for Singapore

Date	N	NE	E	SE	S	SW	W	NW
22nd January	0·814	0·747	0·818	0·813	0·745	0·815	0·815	0·747
22nd February	0·817	0·773	0·824	0·805	0·639	0·807	0·821	0·767
21st March	0·813	0·789	0·822	0·792	0·749	0·789	0·821	0·790
22nd April	0·632	0·804	0·820	0·768	0·811	0·768	0·820	0·805
22nd May	0·730	0·815	0·817	0·747	0·813	0·749	0·817	0·815
22nd June	0·762	0·815	0·814	0·744	0·808	0·712	0·814	0·816
22nd July	0·732	0·814	0·817	0·749	0·813	0·752	0·816	0·813
22nd August	0·636	0·804	0·820	0·772	0·815	0·768	0·820	0·806
24th September	0·814	0·788	0·821	0·791	0·75	0·790	0·821	0·788
21st October	0·817	0·770	0·820	0·808	0·638	0·804	0·823	0·773
22nd November	0·813	0·749	0·816	0·815	0·746	0·815	0·817	0·747
22nd December	0·812	0·741	0·813	0·817	0·777	0·816	0·811	0·739
Annual mean	0·766	0·784	0·818	0·785	0·759	0·782	0·818	0·784

^{a}Normal incidence transmittance of clear glass = 0·874.

Table 7.5
Range of variation of mean solar transmittances of clear glass for Singapore

Orientation	Range of variation	Annual mean value
N	0·632–0·817	0·766
NE	0·741–0·815	0·784
E	0·813–0·824	0·818
SE	0·744–0·817	0·785
S	0·638–0·815	0·759
SW	0·712–0·816	0·782
W	0·811–0·823	0·818
NW	0·739–0·816	0·784

7.6. Solar Control Glasses

A range of special glasses for solar control applications of fenestrations has been developed by major glass manufacturers. These functional glasses have opened up new concepts in building design. The primary function of solar control glasses is to act as an efficient heat filter with little effect on the other functions of the windows such as view and contact, provision of adequate daylight, *etc.* The range of special glasses now available cater for many requirements both in terms of performance and cost. The types of solar control glasses are usually classified under the following broad categories:

(i)   Heat-absorbing glasses.
(ii) Heat-reflecting glasses.
(iii) Photo-chromatic glasses.
(iv) Clear glass treated with heat-reflecting polyester films.

7.6.1. *Heat-Absorbing Glasses*

Heat-absorbing glasses were introduced several decades ago. These glasses are produced by adding small amounts of certain chemicals to the glass melt in the furnace to produce the required tint. When ferrous oxide is added a bluish-green colour will be imparted to the glass. The use of other chemicals like nickel and cobalt oxides and selenium provide a range of colours which include grey and bronze. The tinted and coloured glasses absorb selected parts of solar radiation spectrum throughout the thickness of the glass. These types of glasses absorb a greater part of the infrared with some reduction in the visible light. Heat-absorbing glasses are also produced by a modified float process of glass manufacturing method called spectra float, in which a layer of metal ions is injected first under the surface of the glass ribbons as it is passed through the bath.

The finished product results in a bronze tinted layer just beneath one surface of the glass. Because of its single modified surface layer, the spectra float glass solar control performance is slightly affected by the actual thickness of the glass pane. Grey and coloured glasses reduce solar heat mainly by absorbing the visible part of the solar spectrum. Tinted lacquer treatments have similar characteristics. Glasses which absorb non-selectively throughout the solar spectrum are called 'neutral glasses'. The main drawback of heat-absorbing glasses is that 25–40% of the absorbed heat energy is re-transferred to the interior by

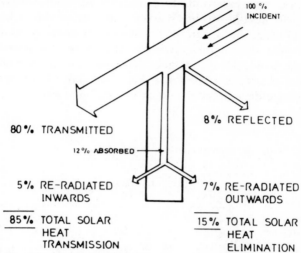

100 % INCIDENT

80 % TRANSMITTED

8 % REFLECTED

12 % ABSORBED

5 % RE-RADIATED INWARDS

7 % RE-RADIATED OUTWARDS

85 % TOTAL SOLAR HEAT TRANSMISSION

15 % TOTAL SOLAR HEAT ELIMINATION

Fig. 7.7. Heat balance diagram for a 3-mm-thick clear glass.

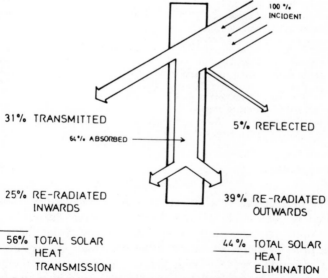

100 % INCIDENT

31 % TRANSMITTED

5 % REFLECTED

64 % ABSORBED

25 % RE-RADIATED INWARDS

39 % RE-RADIATED OUTWARDS

56 % TOTAL SOLAR HEAT TRANSMISSION

44 % TOTAL SOLAR HEAT ELIMINATION

Fig. 7.8. Heat balance diagram for a 6-mm-thick heat-absorbing glass.

convection and radiation. In addition, the high temperatures reached by heat-absorbing glasses exposed to direct sun rays can in practice be a serious source of discomfort to the occupants near the window owing to the thermal radiation from the glass pane. Heat balance diagrams for clear and heat-absorbing glasses are shown in Figs. 7.7 and 7.8, respectively. Performance data for typical heat-absorbing glasses are given in Table 7.6.

Table 7.6
Solar control performance data for heat-absorbing glasses

Description of glass	Light transmission (%)	Total solar heat gain (%)	Shading coefficient (SC)
Single glass			
6-mm clear float	87	84	0·96
6-mm green tinted glass	74	61	0·70
6-mm grey tinted glass	41	61	0·70
6-mm bronze tinted glass	51	61	0.70
6-mm blue–green tinted glass	48	45	0·52
6-mm spectra float bronze glass	50	67	0·77
12-mm grey tinted glass	18	46	0·53
12-mm bronze tinted glass	29	46	0·53
Double glazing (12-mm air space between outer and inner panes)			
3-mm clear glass + 3-mm clear glass	80	72	0·83
6-mm clear glass + 6-mm clear glass	72	73	0·84
6-mm green glass + 6-mm clear glass	63	48	0·55
6-mm grey glass + 6-mm clear glass	35	48	0·55
6-mm bronze glass + 6-mm clear glass	43	48	0·55
6-mm spectral float bronze glass + 6-mm clear glass	42	55	0·63
6-mm grey glass + 6-mm grey glass	17	43	0·49

7.6.2. *Heat-Reflecting Glasses*

The part of the solar spectrum that is reflected by the glass surface is completely excluded from entering the building interior and so does not contribute to the solar heat gain. Reflection is therefore more effective than absorption as a means of reducing solar heat gains. The natural reflectance of ordinary clear sheet or plate glass differs very little from that of

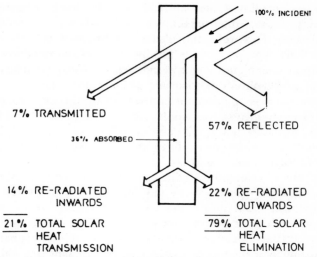

Fig. 7.9. Heat balance diagram for a 6-mm-thick heat-reflecting glass.

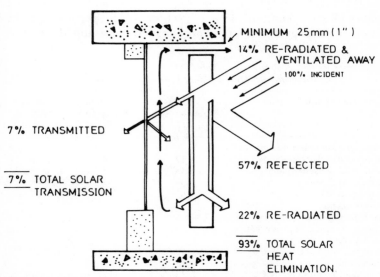

Fig. 7.10. Heat balance diagram for a clear glass window and heat-reflecting glass screen combination.

a transparent tinted heat-absorbing glass. With a metallised reflecting glass, the reflectance of radiation is increased considerably. Heat-reflecting glasses are of comparatively recent origin. This type of glass is produced in an elaborate vacuum deposition technique which produces a microscopically thin layer of pure gold on one surface of clear float glass. Considerable precision is required in controlling the process to ensure uniform coating over the whole area of the pane. A gold wire wound onto a special jig situated between two panes of glass is vaporised at a controlled rate in an evacuated chamber so that the gold mist is deposited as a thin coating accurate to within 0·01 of the wavelength of light. Both gold and azure finishes are produced in the same way by varying the number of depths of the coatings. Gold offers the particular advantage of having excellent reflecting performance in the infrared region of the solar spectrum. Because of this, it is able to reject a substantial part of the solar heat with less loss of visible light transmission. Units of the gold type are capable of rejecting as much as 78% of solar heat. However the azure type rejects about 67% of solar heat while transmitting 47% of visible light. Because of the fragile nature of the coating produced by vacuum deposition

Table 7.7
Solar control performance data for heat-reflecting glasses

Description of glass	Light transmission (%)	Total solar heat gain (%)	Shading coefficient (SC)
Single-glazing laminated glass			
6-mm bronze densely coated	12	24	0·28
6-mm gold densely coated	15	23	0·26
6-mm gold medium coated	38	35	0·40
6-mm gold lightly coated	63	53	0·61
Double glazing			
Inner pane 6-mm clear glass			
(12-mm air space between panes)			
Outer pane			
6-mm bronze densely coated	10	15	0·17
6-mm gold densely coated	13	16	0·18
6-mm gold medium coated	32	27	0·31
6-mm gold lightly coated	58	35	0·40

these heat-reflecting glasses are made available either as double-glazed units in which the coated surface is situated in a protected position on the inside surface of the outer pane, or as a laminated single-glazed unit. In the latter case the panes of glass with a thin vacuum deposited metallic film and clear glass pane are laminated together to protect the reflecting film against abrasion while cleaning and from atmospheric attack. As mentioned earlier the degree of solar heat control, light transmission and glare reduction is governed by the density of the metallic coating deposited on the glass. Heat-reflecting glasses are much more expensive than heat absorbing glasses. Heat balance diagrams for heat-reflecting glass and a clear glass window–heat-reflecting glass screen combination are shown in Figs. 7.9 and 7.10, respectively. Performance data of typical heat-reflecting glasses are given in Table 7.7.

7.6.3. *Photo-Chromatic Glasses*

Photo-chromatic glasses which change their transmittance when exposed to light are a more recent introduction. The active chemical compounds that impart this property to the silicate glasses are silver halide crystals, formed by crystallisation from the glassy matrix during initial cooling or subsequent heat treatment of the glass. The amount of silver is typically 0·5% or less. The crystal size is small compared to the wavelength of light and hence the scattering is not of much concern.

Alkali borosilicates have been found to be, in general, more suitable as the matrix for the photo-chromatic sensitisers.

The suspended crystalline silver halides (silver chloride, silver bromide or both) absorb high-energy photons which dissociate the silver halide. The wavelengths which induce darkening or fading are a continuous spectrum. Photolysis of silver halides may also be sensitised by cuprous ions. The process is reversible. Recovery by recombination occurs by a natural thermal recovery or by interaction with radiation of wavelengths longer than that which darkens the glass. The silver and halogen can return to their original states when the activating light is removed. Spectral transmittances of a typical photo-chromatic glass of 6-mm thickness when unexposed (clear) and exposed to

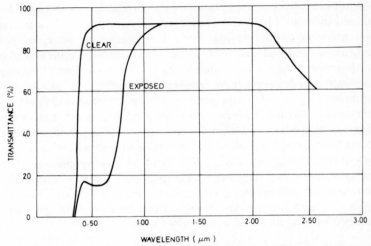

Fig. 7.11.   Spectral transmittance of a typical photo-chromatic glass. (After Smith [7.7]).

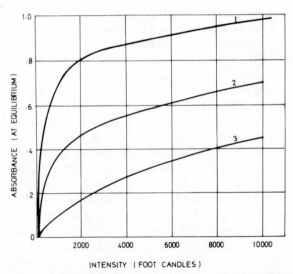

Fig. 7.12.   Effect of light intensity on the absorbance of a few photo-chromatic glasses. (After Smith [7.7]).

sunlight as presented by Smith [7.7] are shown in Fig. 7.11. The glass is transparent when unexposed, darkens to a reasonably neutral grey when exposed to light and clears when the light source is removed. The increase of optical density (darkening) with increase of light intensity and the equilibrium density varies with the glass. Steady-state optical density versus light intensity at constant temperature for three typical photo-chromatic glasses is shown in Fig. 7.12 [7.7]. Both the rate of approach to equilibrium and the equilibrium transmittance are determined by the glass and the temperature of the glass. At lower temperatures, near saturation is achieved at lower levels of intensity. The transmittance increases with increase in temperature for the same level of light intensity and the equilibrium intensity will be higher at higher temperatures of glass as illustrated in Fig. 7.13 [7.7]. The equilibrium temperature of the glass in any particular situation will depend on the total heat gain by absorption and heat loss by conduction, convection and radiation. Thus it can be expected that the performance of these

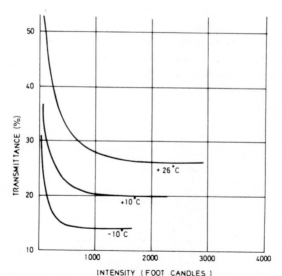

Fig. 7.13. Effect of ambient temperature on transmittance of a photo-chromatic glass. (After Smith [7.7]).

photo-chromatic glasses will be somewhat different for single and double glazing.

When these glasses are used for architectural applications, the following sequence of variation in transmittance over the course of the day can be visualised. They begin to darken at dawn, continue to darken until saturation is achieved, remain darkened throughout the day, begin to clear before sunset and continue to clear at a constantly reducing rate until dawn the next morning. Typical diurnal variation in transmittances of five representative photo-chromatic glasses mounted in a vertical south facing panel are shown in Fig. 7.14 [7.7].

Two important points that can be noted from these curves are (i) the characteristic shape is the same and (ii) the transmittance during the major part of the day remains roughly constant. This latter result may be due to the compensatory effects of light intensity and temperature on the transmittance. That is, as the sunlight intensity increases the transmittance of the glass decreases. However, with the increased intensity the temperature of the glass also increases and the rate of change of transmittance with intensity becomes small, and may be cancelled by the increase in equilibrium transmittance resulting from the increase in the clearing rate of the glass. This has important implications in any design computation of heat gains and light transmission values: a nominal value of transmittance

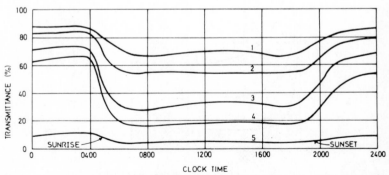

Fig. 7.14. Diurnal variation of transmittance for different photo-chromatic glasses. (After Smith [7.7]).

for the entire day can be used, without introduction of serious errors in the results.

Large diurnal changes in transmittance are possible with photo-chromatic glass. Wide ranges of nominal values may be obtained by selection of the proper glass for any desired amount of light control. Visible transmittance of photo-chromatic glass lies in the range 0·19–0·32 during day-time and 0·59–0·71 during night-time. The shading coefficients may lie in the range of 0·60–0·77. From these figures it is clear that photo-chromatic glass is not promising for solar heat-control applications. It may find limited application where glare control is the prime consideration.

7.6.4. *Solar Control Reflective Polyester-Coated Films*

One of the techniques recently introduced for control of solar heat gain through glass at a lower initial cost than heat reflecting glass, is to apply polyester-coated reflective films to clear glass panes. These films are constructed of a transparent tough polyester sheet film of 0·001–0·002 in. over which a controlled density of aluminium vapour is deposited under vacuum. A further layer of polyester is superimposed to form a sandwich construction. A transparent water-activated and pressure-sensitive adhesive coating is provided for bonding this reflective film to the glass. Variations in the thickness of the film, the density of the aluminium coating, the type of adhesive used and the colour tinting create a range of solar control reflective films with different solar-heat and light-transmission properties. As a rule, heaviest aluminium density films provide the greatest solar heat control (up to 75% reduction) and glare control (up to 82%). Medium and lighter density films give less solar heat and glare reduction but permit greater light transmission. For normal use 0·001-in. thick polyester-film base is used but where extra shatter resistance properties are required, films of 0·002-in. thick are employed. The tints that are normally available for these films are silver, gold, bronze, azure and smoke grey which are obtained by laminating on 0·005-in. film of the appropriate colour onto a thicker layer of the basic film. Further, in these tinted films ultra-violet inhibitors are also incorporated to block the ultra-violet light transmission through the film to a very high degree. Thus they prevent discoloration and fading of clothing, fabrics, draperies, furnishings, *etc.* Perhaps the main advantage of a reflective film is that it can be applied on site to the existing glass in single- or double-glazed windows to convert them as solar control reflective glass without removal of the panes and with least disturbance. It is a much less expensive operation than other forms of reflective glass.

Performance data for solar control films applied to single and double glazing are given in Table 7.8. Sealed double-glazed units incorporating solar control films are now being made. The

Table 7.8
Solar control performance data for reflective-coated polyester films on glass

Description of the reflective film[a]	Ultra-violet light transmission (%)	Daylight transmission (%)	Total solar heat gain (%)	Shading coefficient (SC)
On 3-mm clear glass				
medium-density coat	31	33	34	0·41
heavy-density coat	18	20	21	0·24
On 6-mm heat-absorbing glass				
grey	11	13	33	0·38
bronze	9	16	33	0·38
Ultra-violet inhibited polyester film				
on 3-mm clear glass medium-density reflective coat	1	75	81	0·93
	1	30	37	0·42
heavy-density reflective coat	1	20	28	0·32
Translucent tinted film				
on 3-mm clear glass	1	11	25	0·29
on 6-mm wired glass	1	10	24	0·28
Non-reflective translucent tinted film				
on 3-mm clear glass	1	22	42	0·48
on 6-mm wired glass	1	20	39	0·45

[a] Aluminium-coated polyester film.

reflective film is applied to the inside surface of the external pane. This combines the excellent solar control properties of the reflective film with the improved thermal performance (lower overall thermal transmission coefficients) of double glazing. Double-glazed units have better noise-control properties as well.

7.7. SHADING COEFFICIENTS

For comparing the effective solar control provided by different glazing systems and combinations of glazing and internal and external shading devices, the concept of 'shading coefficient' has been introduced by the American Society of Heating, Refrigeration and Air-conditioning Engineers (ASHRAE) [7.8]. The shading coefficient (SC) is defined as the ratio of the solar heat gain (due to transmission as well as the re-transmitted part of the absorbed radiation) obtained by the combination of the window glass and shading device to that of the solar heat gain through an unshaded clear window glass sheet. Usually a 3-mm clear sheet glass is taken as a standard for this comparison. This may thus be expressed as

$$SC = \frac{\text{solar heat gain (SHG) of any glass and shading combination}}{\text{solar heat gain through a 3-mm unshaded clear glass } (I_{Tg})}$$

The shading coefficient values for different types of glasses, and for a 3-mm clear glass with some common external and internal shading devices are listed in Table 7.9. The shading coefficient values for fixed shading devices like 'sun breakers' will vary according to the percentage of glass areas under shade and exposed to the sun. For time periods when it is fully effective (*i.e.* 100% shading) these have a shading coefficient value of 0·20. At other times, it is necessary to determine the percentage of the shaded and sunlit areas and the corresponding solar heat gain through each part of the window for calculating the effective shading coefficient. Thus for fixed shading systems the shading coefficient also varies with the orientation of the glazed façade. The fraction of window area exposed to sun at any time

Table 7.9

Shading coefficients for different types of glazing and shading devices

Type of glass	Position and type of shading	Shading coefficient (SC)[a]
Clear glass		
3-mm clear glass	none	1·00
6-mm plate glass	none	0·90
Heat-absorbing glass		
6-mm lightly heat-absorbing glass	none	0·51
6-mm densely heat-absorbing glass	none	0·39
6-mm heat absorbing (green)	none	0·67
6-mm heat absorbing (blue)	none	0·55
Heat-reflecting glass		
6-mm heat-reflecting glass (gold)	none	0·24
3-mm clear glass coated with reflecto shield		
RSL-20	none	0·27
RSL-40	none	0·44
6-mm plate glass with thin reflective film linings		
silver	none	0·24–0·28
gold	none	0·26–0·29
grey	none	0·32–0·39
photo-chromatic glasses	none	0·60–0·77
Translucent glass	none	0·57

	external shades	
3-mm clear glass	canvas roller blind	0·14
3-mm clear glass	canvas awnings	0·25
3-mm clear glass	completely shaded by fixed-type sun breakers	0·20
3-mm clear glass	white louvered sun breaker blades at 45°	0·14
3-mm clear glass	venetian blinds, light colour slat angle = 0°	0·10
	= 45°	0·14
	= 90°	0·45

	internal shading	
	roller shades	
3-mm clear glass	(a) white colour	0·40
3-mm clear glass	(b) medium colour	0·62
3-mm clear glass	heavy curtain with white lining and folds	0·35
3-mm clear glass	net curtain with folds (dark)	0·75
3-mm clear glass	venetian blinds, light colour slat angle = 0°	0·50
3-mm clear glass	= 45°	0·63
3-mm clear glass	= 90°	0·78

[a]These are typical values only. Variations will occur due to variations in type and colour of glass, differences in treatments, cleanliness of glass and shading devices.

for a given orientation due to a fixed louvre system can be determined by the methods discussed in Chapter 3. Once the fraction of exposed area is determined, the net shading coefficient (SC′) for a partially shaded window (for that time and orientation) can be obtained by

$$SC' = \frac{A_1 \times I_{Dg} + fAI_{dg}}{A \times I_{Tg}} \qquad (7.20)$$

where SC′ is the net shading coefficient for a partially shaded window; I_{Tg} is the total (direct and diffuse) solar radiation transmitted through standard 3-mm clear glass for that orientation (called the solar heat-gain factor, SHGF); I_{Dg} is the direct solar radiation transmitted through standard 3-mm clear glass; I_{dg} is the diffuse solar radiation transmitted; A_1 is the area of the window exposed to sun; A is the total window area; and f is the fraction of diffuse radiation obstructed by the shading device.

If the glass used is not the standard 3-mm clear glass but heat-absorbing or heat-reflecting glass or clear glass treated with solar reflective film and/or in combination with internal shading devices, the overall effective shading coefficient for the system (SC″) can be obtained by multiplying the shading coefficient for the partially shaded window clear glass (SC′) with corresponding shading coefficient of the glass and/or internal shading device combination (SC), *i.e.* SC″ = SC′ × SC.

The actual solar heat gain (SHG) through a fenestration of a given orientation with a sun-control device for the required time can be obtained as SHG = I_{Tg} × SC″. Total heat gain (THG) through the fenestration includes the conducted heat through the glazing due to the temperature difference between outdoor and indoor conditions. This is given as THG = SHG + $U_g(t_o - t_i)$ where t_o is the outdoor air temperature, t_i is the indoor air temperature, and U_g is the U value of the glazing system.

7.8. Solar Calorimeter

Solar optical properties of glass specimens can be determined by means of a pyrheliometer which measures transmittance and reflectance for solar radiation at varying incident angles. For more complicated fenestrations with combination of shading devices, a solar calorimeter is used [7.9]; the ASHRAE research laboratories at Cleveland designed a solar calorimeter for this purpose. This consists of a well-insulated semi-cylindrical heat-absorbing unit with a 4-ft square opening. The test specimen is fitted into the opening. The absorbing surface is a lamp-black-coated copper plate to which copper cooling coils are blazed. A coolant liquid is circulated through the coils which picks up the heat absorbed by the plate and maintains a constant temperature within the calorimeter. The temperature rise of the coolant between the inlet and outlet points is measured by a thermopile made up of 24 junctions of thermocouples. The flow rate of the coolant is also measured from a knowledge of the specific heat of the coolant, the total heat gains through the fenestration under test can be determined. Heat loss through the

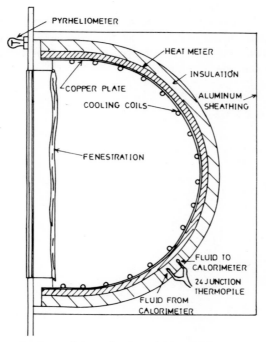

Fig. 7.15. Schematic view of solar calorimeter.

supporting framework and the insulation at the back of the absorber unit are measured by means of heat flow meters. This includes the heat transfer due to outside and inside air temperature difference across the fenestration. To separate the solar heat gains from the total heat gains through the fenestration, the U value of the system is to be determined separately. A schematic view of the solar calorimeter is shown in Fig. 7.15. The calorimeter unit is mounted on a table which can be tilted up to 90° in the vertical plane and is rotatable through 360° in the horizontal plane.

An alternative procedure for determining the solar heat gains alone *i.e.* directly transmitted plus part of the absorbed portion that is re-transmitted to inside space, is to measure the solar transmittance by means of a pyrheliometer and the temperature rise of the panel above the inside space by means of thermocouples. From these measured values of solar transmittance and temperature rise the overall solar heat-gain factor can be computed. This method is simple and inexpensive compared to the solar calorimeter method and provides reasonably accurate results. From the test results by either method the shading coefficients can be obtained.

References

Chapter 1

1.1. FLETCHER, SIR B., *A History of Architecture on the Comparative Method*, Batsford, London, 1956.
1.2. METCALF, R. AND METCALF, O., *Making Stained Glass*, David & Charles Ltd., 1972. *a*, p. 16; *b*, p. 17.
1.3. RAEBURN, M., *An Outline of World Architecture*, Octopus Books Ltd., London, 1973.
1.4. MCGRATH, R. AND FROST, A. C., *Glass in Architecture and Decoration*, The Architectural Press, London, 1961. *a*, p. 28; *b*, p. 30; *c*, p. 36; *d*, p. 39; *e*, pp. 41, 42; *f*, p. 42; *g*, pp. 45, 46; *h*, pp. 153–6; *i*, 49–59.
1.5. BETJEMAN, J., *A Pictorial History of English Architecture*, Penguin Books, England.
1.6. CHAMBERS, SIR W., *A Treatise on the Decorative Part of Civil Architecture*, first published, London, 1791; revised 1968, Benjamin Blom, Bronx, New York. *a*, p. 115; *b*, p. 116.
1.7. HIX, J., *The Glass House*, Phaidon Press Ltd., 1974. *a*, p. 12; *b*, p. 19; *c*, p. 45; *d*, p. 146.
1.8. PEPTON, H., *Fragments on the Theory and Practice of Landscape Gardening*, 1816. See ref. 1.4, p. 157.
1.9. TANT, B., *Glass Architecture*, Praeger Publishers, New York, 1972. *a*, p. 14; *b*, p. 571. An introductory essay by Dennis Sharp is included.
1.10. GROPIUS, W., *The New Architecture and the Bauhaus*, London, pp. 22–23, 1937.
1.11. GIEDION, S., *Space, Time, and Architecture*, Harvard University Press, p. 616, 1967.
1.12. HITCHCOCK, H. R., *Architecture of the 19th and 20th Centuries*, Penguin Books, England.
1.13. HAYNES, E. B., *Glass through the Ages*, Pelican Books, 1959.

Chapter 2

2.1. KIMBALL, H. H. and HAND, I. F., 'Sky-brightness and daylight-illumination measurements', *Mon.-Weath. Rev.*, Wash., **49**, 1921, 481.
2.2. HOPKINSON, R. G., 'Measurements of sky luminance distribution at Stockholm', *J. Opt. Soc. Amer.*, **44**, 1954, 455. Quoted by Hopkinson, R. G., Petherbridge, P. and Longmore, J., *Daylighting*, Heinemann, London, p. 57, 1966.
2.3. NARASIMHAN, V., *The Illumination Climate and the Design of Openings for Daylighting of School Buildings in South East Asia and Ceylon*, study 13, Asian Regional Institute for School Building Research (sponsored by UNESCO), Colombo, 1970.

2.4.   MOON, P. and SPENCER, D. E., 'Illumination from a non-uniform sky', *Illum. Eng.*, **37**, 1942, 707.

2.5.   HOPKINSON, R. G., PETHERBRIDGE, P. and LONGMORE, J., *Daylighting*, Heinemann, London, 1966. *a*, p. 42; *b*, p. 46; *c*, p. 47; *d*, p. 54.

2.6.   RENNHACKKAMP, W. H. M., *Sky Luminance Distribution in Warm Climate*, Compte Rendu, Commission Internationale de l'Eclairage, Washington, June 1967, p. 465.

2.7.   LYNES, J. A., *Principles of Natural Lighting*, Applied Science Publishers Ltd., 1968. *a*, p. 61; *b*, p. 60.

2.8.   THE ILLUMINATING ENGINEERING SOCIETY (LONDON), *IES Code: Interior Lighting*, p. 57, 1977.

2.9.   *Interior Lighting Design*, 3rd edn., Lighting Industry Federation Ltd., UK, p. 57, 1970.

2.10. COMMISSION INTERNATIONAL DE L'ECLAIRAGE, *International Lighting Vocabulary*, Bureau Central de la CIE, Paris Publication CIE No. 17 (E-11), p. 226, 1970.

2.11. HOPKINSON, R. G., LONGMORE, J. and PETHERBRIDGE, P., 'An empirical formula for the computation of the indirect component of daylight factor', *Trans. Illum. Eng. Soc. (London)*, **19**, 1954, 201.

2.12. PHILIPS, R. O., Faculty of Architecture, University of New South Wales, Sydney, Australia.

2.13. LONGMORE, J., 'BRS daylight protractors', Department of the Environment/Building Research Station, HMSO London, 1968.

2.14. HOPKINSON, R. G., LONGMORE, J., and GRAHAM, A. M., 'Simplified daylight tables', National Building Studies, special report No. 26, Department of Scientific and Industrial Research (Building Research Station), HMSO London, 1958.

2.15. 'Daytime lighting in buildings', Illuminating Engineering Society, technical report No. 4, IES, London, July 1972.

Chapter 3

3.1.   OLGYAY, A. and OLGYAY, V., *Solar Control and Shading Devices*, Princeton University Press, 1957.

3.2.   P. BURBERRY (ed.), 'The sun. 2. Geometry of sunlight'. *The Architects Journal*, January 12, 1966, 109–131.

3.3.   'Sunlight 4', *The Architects Journal*, October 23, 1968, 963–8; 'Sunlight 5', *The Architects Journal*, October 30, 1968, 1019–36.

3.4.   RICHARDS, S. J., *Solar Charts for the Design of Sunlight and Shade for Buildings in South Africa*, National Building Research Institute, Pretoria, 1952.

3.5.   PETHERBRIDGE, P., 'Sunpath diagrams and overlays for solar heat gain calculations', *BRS Current Papers*, Building Research Station (UK), research series No. 39, March 1965.

3.6.   PHILIPS, R. O., 'Sunshine and shade in Australia', Commonwealth Experimental Building Station, Australia, Bulletin No. 8, 1963.

3.7.   SPENCER, J. W., 'Calculation of solar position for building purposes', Division of Building Research, Technical paper No. 14, CSIRO, Australia.

3.8. SESHADRI, T. N., RAO, K. R. *et al., Climatological and Solar Data for India*, Central Building Research Institute, Roorkee, India, 1969.

Chapter 4

4.1. ABBOT, C. G. *et al., Annals of the Astrophysical Observatory of the Smithsonian Institution*, Washington D.C., **2** (1908); **3** (1913); **4** (1922); **5** (1932); **6** (1942).
4.2. JOHNSON, F. S., 'The solar constant', *J. Meteorology*, **11**(6), December 1954, 431–9.
4.3. THEKAEKARA, M. P., 'Proposed standard values of the solar constant and the solar spectrum', *J. Environmental Sciences*, **13**(4), 1970, 6–9.
4.4. MOON, P., 'Proposed standard solar radiation curves for engineering use', *J. Franklin Inst.*, **230**, 1940, 583–617.
4.5. FRITZ, S., 'Solar radiation during cloudless days', *Heat Vent.*, **46**(1), 1949, 69–74. *a*, p. 238, 240; *b*, 69–74.
4.6. THERLKELD, J. L. and JORDAN, R. C., 'Direct solar radiation available on clear days', *Heat Pip. Air-cond.*, **29**(12), 1957, 135–145.
4.7. WESLEY, M. L. and LIPSCHUTZ, R. C., 'A method for estimating hourly average of diffuse and direct solar radiation under a layer of scattered clouds', *Solar Energy*, **18**, 1976, 467–73.
4.8. RAO, K. R. and SESHADRI, T. N., 'Solar insolation curves'. *Indian J. Met. & Geophysics*, **12**(2), 1961, 267–72.
4.9. SPENCER, J. W., 'Estimation of solar radiation in Australian localities on clear days', Division of Building Research, technical paper No. 15, 1965, CSIRO, Australia.
4.10. SPENCER, J. W., 'Computer estimation of solar radiation on clear days', *Solar Energy*, **13**, 1972, 437–8.
4.11. SPENCER, J. W., 'Solar position and radiation tables for Sydney (latitude 34°S)', Division of Building Research Reports, 1968, CSIRO, Australia.
4.12. ASHRAE (USA), *Handbook of Fundamentals*, Ch. 22, American Society of Heating, Refrigeration and Air-Conditioning Engineers, 1972.
4.13. IHVE GUIDE (UK), *Book A. Design Data*, Institute of Heating and Ventilating Engineers, UK, 1970.
4.14. SPENCER, J. W., 'Solar position and radiation tables for, Sydney, Melbourne, Perth, Adelaide, Brisbane, Darwin...', Division of Building Research Reports, 1968, CSIRO, Australia.
4.15. SESHADRI, T. N., RAO, K. R. *et al., Climatological and Solar Data for India* (to design buildings for thermal comfort), Central Building Research Institute, Roorkee, India, 1969.
4.16. PARMELEA, G., 'Irradiation of vertical and horizontal surfaces by diffuse solar radiation from cloudless skies', *Trans. ASHRAE*, **60**, 1954, 341.
4.17. LIU, B. Y. and JORDAN, R. C., 'The inter-relationship and characteristic distribution of direct, diffuse and total solar radiation', *Solar Energy*, **3**, 1960, 1–19.
4.18. BALLANTYNE, E. R., 'Solar tables and diagrams for building designers', in: *Proceedings of CIE Conference on Sunlight in Buildings*, June 1967, Rotterdam, Vol. 1, No. 20, pp. 251–64.

4.19. PENWARDEN, A. D., Unpublished note, Building Research Station (UK), 1962.
4.20. LOUDON, A. G., 'The interpretation of solar radiation measurements for building problems', Building Research Station (UK), research paper 73, August 1967.
4.21. ANGSTRON, A., 'On computation of global radiation from the records of sunshine', *Arkiv. Geophysik*, **3**(23), 1956, 557–66.
4.22. BLACK, J. N. *et al.*, 'Solar radiation and duration of sunshine' *Quart. J.R. Met. Soc.*, **80**, 1954, 231–5.
4.23. RAMDAS, L. A. and YEGNANNARAYAMA, S., 'Solar energy in India', *Proceedings of the New Delhi Symposium on Wind and Solar Energy*, UNESCO, p. 188, 1956.
4.24. ROBINSON, N., *Solar Radiation*, Elsevier, Amsterdam, 1966.
4.25. GARG, H. P., 'Application of solar energy for water heater and room heating', Ph.D. Thesis, University of Roorkee, Roorkee, 1972.
4.26. ORGILL, J. F. and HOLLANDS, K. G. T., 'Correlation equation for hourly diffuse radiation on a horizontal surface', *Solar Energy*, **19**, 1977, 357–9.
4.27. SHARMA, M. R. and RAO, K. R., 'Solar radiation protractors', *N.B.O. Journal*, **IV**, NOA, October 1959, 3–12.
4.28. PETHERBRIDGE, P., 'Sunpath diagrams and overlays for solar heat gain calculations', *BRS Current Papers*, Building Research Station (UK), research series No. 39, March 1965.

Chapter 5

5.1.   'Wind loads', *BSI British Standards Code of Practice CP3*, Ch. V, part 2, British Standards Institution, London, 1972.
5.2.   NEWBERRY, C. W. and EATON, K. J., 'Wind loading handbook', Building Research Establishment Report, 1974.
5.3.   'Glazing and fixing of glass for buildings', *BSI British Standards Code of Practice, CP152:1972*, British Standards Institution, London, 1972.
5.4.   *BSI DD4 Recommendation for the Grading of Windows* (resistance to wind loads, air infiltration and water penetration, and with notes on window security), London, 1971.
5.5.   SHAND, E. B., *Glass Engineering Handbook*, McGraw-Hill, 1958.
5.6.   BOWLES, R. and SUGARMAN, B., 'The strength and deflection characteristics of large rectangular panels under uniform pressure', *Glass Technology*, **3**(5), October 1962.
5.7.   MAYNE, J. R. and WALKER, G. R., 'The response of glazing to wind pressure', Building Research Establishment, current paper No. 44, June 1976.
5.8.   KHAN, F. R., 'Optimum design of glass in buildings', *Building Research*, May–June, 1967.
5.9.   TIMOSHENKO, S. and WOINOWSKY-KRIEGER, S., *Theory of Plates and Shells*, McGraw-Hill, 1959.
5.10. MARCUS, H., *Die Theorie elastischer Gewebe* (The Theory of the Elastic Grid), Vol. I, Springer, Berlin, 1932.

5.11. LAWSON, T. V. and PENWARDEN, A. D., 'The effects of wind on people in the vicinity of buildings', in: *Proceedings of the Fourth International Conference on Wind Effects on Buildings and Structures*, Heathrow, 1975.
5.12. BECKETT, H. E. and GODFREY, J. A., *Windows: Performance, Design and Installation*, Crosby Lockwood Staples, London, 1974.
5.13. CROFT, D. D. and HOOPER, J. A., 'The Sydney Opera House', *The Structural Engineer*, 51(9), September 1973.

Chapter 6

6.1. DOELLE, L. L., *Environmental Acoustics*, McGraw-Hill, 1972.
6.2. SMITH, B. J., *Environmental Physics—Acoustics*, Longman, 1971.
6.3. PILKINGTON BROTHERS LTD., *Windows and Environment*, first published in 1971 by the Architectural Press on behalf of the Pilkington Environmental Advisory Service.
6.4. SOUND RESEARCH LABORATORIES LTD., *Practical Building Acoustics*, 1970.
6.5. MATTAR, A. B. M., 'The acoustics of tropical windows', M.A. Thesis, Sheffield University, 1971.

Chapter 7

7.1. YELLOT, J. I., 'How materials react to solar energy. Part 2. Characteristics of glass and glass shading', *Architectural Record*, June 1966, 197.
7.2. PARMELEA, G. V., 'Heat transmission through glass', *ASHVE Research Bulletin*, 53(1), July 1947.
7.3. MITALAS, G. P. and STEPHENSON, D. G., *Absorption and Transmission of Thermal Radiation by Single and Double Glazed Windows*, National Research Council, Canada, Division of Building Research, NRC 7104, December 1962.
7.4. SPENCER, J. W., 'Estimation of solar radiation in Australian localities on clear days', Division of Building Research, technical paper No. 15, CSIRO, Australia, 1965.
7.5. STEPHENSON, D. G., 'Equations for solar heat gain through windows', *Solar Energy*, 9(2), 1965, 81–6.
7.6. PETHERBRIDGE, P., 'Transmission characteristics of window glasses and sun controls', Building Research Station (UK) research paper No. 72, October 1967.
7.7. SMITH, G. P., 'Thermal performance of photochromatic glasses', *Building Research*, May–June 1967, 24–9.
7.8. *ASHRAE Handbook of Airconditioning Fundamentals*, 1967.
7.9. PENNINGTON, C. W., *et al.*, 'Experimental analysis of solar heat gain through insulating glass with indoor shading', University of Florida, technical paper No. 281, April 1964.

Index

255

I

F